Worst
Fashions

Colourful crinkly acrylics were
always best avoided.

Worst
Fashions

What we shouldn't
have worn . . . but did

CATHERINE
HORWOOD

SUTTON PUBLISHING

First published in 2005 by
Sutton Publishing Limited · Phoenix Mill
Thrupp · Stroud · Gloucestershire · GL5 2BU

British Library Cataloguing in Publication Data
A catalogue record for this book is available from the British Library.

ISBN 0 7509 4159 6

Half-title picture: Forest green and purple paisley, *c.* 1970.

Page design by Glad Stockdale.

Typeset in 15/20 Myriad Tilt.
Typesetting and origination by
Sutton Publishing Limited.
Printed and bound in England by
J.H. Haynes & Co. Ltd, Sparkford.

Contents

The wool-like texture is just one reason you'll like these acrylic knits. Here are four more:

4.59 each
Any 2 for 9.00

- Fully fashioned for better fit
- Bounce-back-knits keep their shape
- Machine wash and dry
- Excellent value—save on two

7 to 9 Springy acrylic knit pullovers are well-mannered wardrobe extenders you'll wear and wear. Long, raglan-style sleeves are full fashioned for bind-free comfort. Sizes S (36-inch chest), M (38-40), L (42-44), XL (46).

(7) Three-button placket style with contrast trim on waistband, collar and cuffs. *Colours: order by number and name.* 34—olive; 45—med. blue; 66—cinnamon.
28-E 5359BS—Each................ 4.59

(8) Round-about stripes on body and cuffs of this mock turtle style. Solid-colour sleeves. *Colours: order by number and name.* 45—med. blue; 66—cinnamon; 34—olive.
28-E 5361BS—Each................ 4.59

(9) Mock turtleneck style with contrast stripe on neckband, waistband and cuffs. *Colours: order by number and name.* 66—cinnamon; 48—navy; 34—olive.
28-E 5360BS—Each................ 4.59

Even better value—any 2 for 9.00

Synthetics and sweaters never were a winning combination.

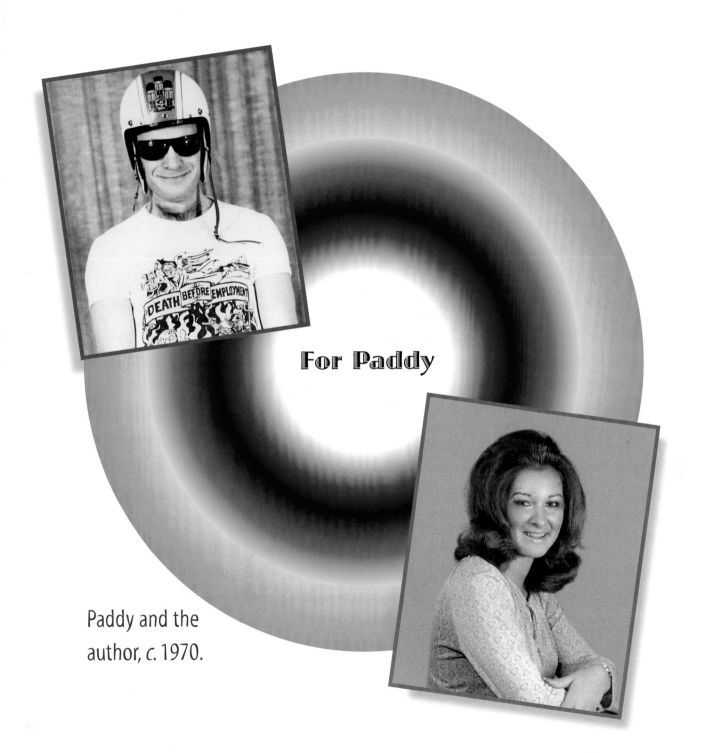

For Paddy

Paddy and the
author, *c.* 1970.

Introduction

This book presents a selection of the worst fashions from the last fifty years. It is admittedly subjective; there is no textbook or theory to say which are the best or worst fashions. Yet ask anyone about their most embarrassing fashion memories and they can recall them instantly: 20- and 30-something women groan at leg warmers and boob tubes they wore at school discos in the 1980s, 40-something men remember going to 'uni' in flares and platforms in the 1970s, and even a few grannies look longingly at the lime-green hot pants they wore in their youth and wonder where the years went.

What makes one fashion 'worse' than another? Oscar Wilde said 'fashion is a form of ugliness so intolerable that we have to alter it every six months'. But last year's outfits don't necessarily qualify for 'worst'; they're just out of fashion. For something to count as bad fashion it must send shivers of embarrassment down our spines. It usually takes several years to achieve this status, just in time for it to be rediscovered and become part of the fashion cycle once more.

Does this mean that we will all be wearing the fashions in this book again? In most cases, no, but there's a twist. While it is true that 'every generation laughs at the old fashions, but follows religiously the new', there are fewer and fewer truly new fashions around. The strict rules that dictated that skirts had to be short or long, trousers narrow or wide, have relaxed enormously over the last few years. Fashion now is eclectic, cherry-picking the best and sometimes the worst from past years.

In the 1950s, a new generation of designers was taken up by a new generation of young consumers. By the 1960s, the influence of haute couture was declining and instead it became impossible to separate fashion from popular music. Famous – and in some cases infamous – pop singers and rock groups wore some of the most over-the-top outfits of the 1970s and 1980s, and you will find many of them illustrated here. While few fans dressed directly to emulate their musical heroes, the influence of groups such as The Beatles with their long hair and round glasses and The Kinks with their frilly shirts in the 1960s helped to make these and other pop fashions acceptable and mainstream.

Cringe-worthy clothes often come to symbolise a particular era. Groups such as Slade, Abba and the Sex Pistols helped to create the extreme styles of the mid- to late 1970s. Just the names conjure up visions of crazy platform boots, electric blue knickerbockers, and punk rips and safety pins. Movies and television programmes also had their influence. We have *Bonnie and Clyde* to thank for a brief outburst of berets in 1967. Throughout the 1980s, the Dynasty-style, padded shoulder power suit was a hot fashion style, but it suddenly seemed inappropriate when the financial bubble burst at the end of the decade.

New artificial fibres and fabrics have also changed the feel and look of clothes over the last fifty years – some for the better, some definitely for the worse. Crimplene may be found only in the charity shop now, but elastane, better known as Lycra, has changed the way we dress everyday, especially for sport, and few of us would want to be without it. Other materials have followed Crimplene into obscurity.

There are also the fads and crazes that take hold in classrooms and clubs, only to be dropped by their fickle fans a few months later – where now Hypercolour t-shirts and mood rings?

So you admit to wearing some of these fashions? Don't worry. You are not the only one. Just remember, 'good taste is better than bad taste but bad taste is better than no taste'.

The author at the height – or should that be depth? – of fashion, 1970s.

Sad Slacks

Not so Relieved   Button Flies

If you're a woman, you probably won't have given it much thought, but be honest – accessibility is a major concern in men's trousers. So in the 1930s when King George V replaced his button flies with a zip fastener, he was only doing what thousands of other men were keen to do as well – go for the quick-and-easy option. No more fumbling with awkward buttonholes, a quick zip and there you were.

Then what happened in the 1960s? Some bright spark thought it would be a good idea to bring back the button fly. And not only that, on the outside and preferably on hipster trousers. Did they really think that this was a step forward? Or attractive to women? Was this supposed to be a come-hither look? Never.

A fashion reversal that was not to be recommended, 1970.

Even new button flies looked unfortunate, 1970.

It always looked tacky and cheap, and on the worst pairs, it gaped. Yet for a few years, it was a stable fixture whether on polyester pants or drainpipe denims – and the tighter the better. But once the hippie look passed and pop stars became more prosperous this was one fashion that disappeared never to return.

It's rare that something made a tank top look good but button flies did, 1970s.

An Overall Mistake

Dungarees for women

Back in 2003, there was a nasty fashion moment when the dreaded 'd' word started appearing in shops again from New Bond Street to the New King's Road. Dungarees made a brief reappearance with labels as high class as Ralph Lauren, Joseph and even Alberta Ferretti inside them. Dungarees instantly conjure up images of the worst of the 1970s. Silly celebrity wearers recently included 'should-have-known-better' Jennifer Aniston and 'this-is-one-craze-I-won't-get going'

Sarah Jessica Parker. The tight ones were not designed with women with anything more than a B-cup in mind. Even Diana, Princess of Wales managed to look silly wearing a pair at a polo match in Windsor in the 1980s.

In contrast, the baggy ones bring back memories of feminist protest marches and at the very least of Felicity Kendal in *The Good Life*, trowel in hand and speck of

Silly dots and stripes complete this clown-look dungaree outfit, 1972.

12

ROMP-IN

Unspeakably unpatriotic red, white and blue bib and braces, 1970s.

Purple jersey horrors complete with the Princess Leia-look hairstyle, 1970.

soil on her golden hair, or Helena Bonham Carter during her 1980s grunge phase. Then there are the 'show-off-your-bump' maternity dungarees complete with bib. If this is to get mum in the mood for the years of striped Osh Kosh B'Gosh dungarees the newborn will be wearing, then it is a mistake. Bibs are for babies, not mummies, however yummy.

DODGY Decorators

Dungarees for men

Maybe if you are panning for gold in the Yukon or stacking corn in Ohio then denim dungarees are just the job. But walking down Chelsea's King's Road in the 1970s was not quite the same thing. Depending on your generation, they just bring back memories of Jeb Clampett from *The Beverley Hillbillies* or John Boy in *The Waltons*.

At least they all wore the baggy workman's overall variety, not the crotch-gripping style that literally took hold of many men in the 1970s.

Pop stars led the way with this comical style. David Bowie has worn many dodgy outfits over the

Chelsea footballer Alan Hudson and friends in Mr Freedom's dungaree choices, 1973.

14

Ronnie Wood ready for a spot of painting and decorating in St Tropez, 1976.

If only he had seen himself from the back, 1973.

the 1970s, Elton John, who reputedly wore them with a mink coat, mink-trimmed glasses and no shirt. Sorry, Sir Elton, that little boy look just did not wash. Men's dungarees are best left to Bob the Builder.

years. In 1974, he even admitted to wearing green dungarees in teen magazine *Mirabelle*, and his red dungarees around that time weren't much better. Seen in St Tropez in the 1970s, Ronnie Wood also looked exceedingly silly in his denim dungarees. And Rod Stewart's ex, Britt Ekland, was blamed for his silky dungaree phase. But none of them looked quite as stupid as the most ludicrous dungaree wearer of

Flapping in the Wind

Carnaby Street – birthplace of the flares phenomenon, 1960s.

Flares for men

Funny how just the word 'flares' sets a whole generation on nostalgia trips remembering kipper ties, polyester shirts and all the other ghastlies that mark out the 1970s as the worst dressed decade of the twentieth century. This was no hippy look – the flowers and the embroidery were long gone. Flares were the new trouser shape for every man – even your dad realised he had to have trousers that flared out from the knee similar to but definitely not a bellbottom, preferably in some awful synthetic mixture. It is their ubiquity that marks out flares as the

Carnaby Flares

Trousers for guys and chicks as we make for the top groups. High waisted hip and top leg hugging, flared to any bottom up to 26". Custom built to your own measurements so state waist, hip, top leg, inside leg, & bottoms rqd. Cols. Navy, Black, Tan and Green. (Plain or Herringbone.)

99'6 p.p. 4/6

Send S.A.E. for 1970 Leaflet.
CARNABY CAVERN (Dept. RVB2)
6 Ganton Street (off Carnaby St.)
London W1A 4QC

£49·99
£1·32
for 38 wks

REAL SUEDE

trouser horror of the decade. Everyone wore them, whatever age, class or sex, men in suits, students in denim or disco divas. Suddenly they were out – leaving behind a wardrobe full of memories never to be brought out again – except as a joke. The confessions of 1970s pop journalist Charles Shaar

Stripes before the eyes and hideous high-waisters, 1978.

Drink a toast to the height of flare fashion, 1974.

Murray sum up their silliness: 'It wasn't until I ditched my last pair of flares shortly before the onset of punk that I realised that there was no law of nature which decreed that trouser bottoms must always be wet and muddy.' Common sense reigned again.

17

OFF PISTE — OR PISTE OFF

Ski pants

Worst Women's
7
Fashions

These weren't flattering even from the front and never will be, 1989.

St Moritz, Courcheval, Verbier, it's a jet-set world out there on the ski slopes where *glühwein* and fur coats are de rigueur and it's social death to wear last year's outfits. When you struggle off-piste, however, you would normally leave those pants behind. But in the 1980s, comfort was key and there was nothing more comfortable than sloping off to the shops in a pair of ski pants. With their instep-grapping straps and bum-clutching tightness, these are the sort of pants that look stunning on a 5ft 10in model with legs like a giraffe. On anyone else there was no escaping the fact that they were incredibly unflattering, especially from behind. Before long, the knees began to bag unless they had got so much elastane in them they turned sitting down into a thigh-strengthening exercise.

It was one thing wearing these trousers tucked into a pair of furry moon boots, but to wear them with shoes, or even worse, stilettos, was one of the naffest looks of the 1980s. No-one wanted to see all that black elastic strapping. These trousers should be sent back to the piste where they belong.

Dishonourable Mentions

Embroidered jeans
hearts and flowers
on your legs

The ultimate no-no – ski pants with stilettos, 1980.

CURTAIN MATERIAL STRIDES

Patterned trousers

It would be nice to think that some of these patterned trousers were a joke. Did men really want to wear fabric that looked as though it had been hanging up as curtains in a caravan? Sadly they did. In the 1960s, in particular, patterns were everywhere. Op Art and Pop Art produced some hideously colourful and in-your-face designs spurred on by the psychedelic hippie movement and work such as that by Beatle cover artist Peter Blake.

Unfortunately some of these patterns seem to have ended up on men's legs. If they were worn with long hair, a bandana, beads and a tie-dye t-shirt then maybe it could be put down to youthful exuberance or a bit too much 'wacky backy'. But to wear loud patterned trousers in the

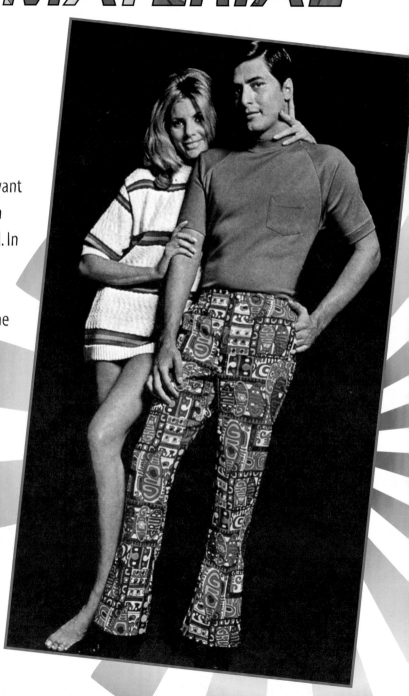

The jumper may have looked better on her but the trousers wouldn't, 1970s.

Horoscope horrors predict a tall, dark pratt, 1970s.

cold light of day without the slightest hint of irony was inexcusable. Was this a reaction against years of grey flannel? Or just fashion fabric madness? Whatever, it did not take hold for long on either side of the Atlantic.

Big Brother baddy Nick Chapman showing his taste matches his character, 2000.

100% cotton screened print "Horoscope" fun slacks and 50% Dacron Polyester/50% cotton Flares. Styled for action.

175 cc 4-stroke OHC twin-cylinder. Top speed 80 mph.

100% female. Spirited performer. Runs cool. Quick response.

Carsuals®

Get into high gear. Scramble into a pair of "Horoscope" fun slacks with popular stove-pipe legs. Or green flares with woven stripes and rounded Western front pockets. Wide range of other patterns. Cuffless—permanent press. At better selected stores. About $9.00.

LOONY LOONS

Bellbottoms

Worst Men's **5** Fashions

In 2002, a headmaster sent a dozen girls home from school in Oxfordshire after he claimed that their enormously wide trousers were a safety hazard. How appropriate that the nearest thing fashion has seen this century that resembles the 1920s trouser craze, the Oxford bag, should cause such a stir eighty years later in the same county from which it emanated.

Whether it was Oxford bags, bellbottoms or 'loons', from the late 1960s to the mid-1970s, plenty will remember that only 28in bottoms on their trousers would do. David Thomas, now a staid 40-something writer, remembers owning in 1976, 'a pair of cream-coloured Oxford bags ... that

White bags and a girl on your arm – did he have it all in 1974?

FASHION FACTS

The ultimate recycled fabric is fleece. Made from recycled plastic bottles, in 1999 fleece was named as one of Time *magazine's 'hundred great inventions of the twentieth century'. However, unlike natural fabrics, it will last as long as the plastic bottles from which it is made.*

were impressively voluminous, all the way from waist to foot.' In addition, he asks to have taken into consideration, 'several pairs of cheap cotton loonpants … these wildly flared monstrosities, in a variety of unbecoming colours, were bought from small ads at the back of the *New Musical Express* and could be guaranteed to split like a rotten tomato at the slightest provocation … by the summer of '77, the wearing of flared denim was an admission that you were a sad, old hippie'. By the 1980s, only the loony wore 'loons'.

Top jean label Wrangler went to great widths to show it was 'with it', 1970s.

Cotton loons were cheap and came in every colour of the rainbow, 1960s.

SAD, PLAID AND DANGEROUS TO KNOW
Checked trousers

Unfortunately, when men try to do 'coloured casual' it never quite comes off. The worst were those who tried to be just a little bit adventurous. They knew that subtle checks were okay for suits and pants so why not go just a little bit further and add some colour? Because it screamed out 'naff', that's why. But in the 1970s, you couldn't move in a man's clothes shop for the most hideous variety of polyester plaid trousers and shirts.

The most famous check, the Burberry beige, black and red version, has been around since the 1920s, and used to be a symbol of smart

Even on a dull day, you couldn't have missed the chap on the right, 1970s.

sophistication. All that might change now. The latest group to go crazy for it are the 'chavs', young, British, white, working-class and usually unemployed. Not that it worries Burberry's Chief Executive, American Rose Marie Bravo: 'You can sell to the customers, but the way they put it together is their own style. We can't dictate who can wear it or how they will wear it. And,

Elton John at the Burberry check-in at Heathrow, 2000.

The first mate's checks should have been reported to the captain, 1970s.

at the end of the day, if it's the real thing, it is still a sale.' With luck, the chavs will move on to something else. It has remained the 'B' – and sometimes even the 'A' – list celebrity's check of choice for years.

25

The Long and the Broad of it

Palazzo pants

In the early 1970s, women's trousers got wider and wider. And not just trousers. Culottes got longer and wider as well and should have come with a public health warning. Have you ever tried walking down a flight of stairs in the 'palazzo pant' look? It may have been undignified to hitch them to the knees but unless you did, you were liable to end up in an even more undignified heap at the bottom instead. But with masses of cheap, bright, garish synthetic fabrics about, the temptation for designers to copy the silk creations of Italian designer Pucci, with his wildly extravagant trouser widths, was too much to resist. The other problem was that synthetics clung like mad, so if they were not dangerously flapping round your ankles, then they were unflatteringly clinging to your thighs.

Any resemblance to bellbottoms is not coincidental. This is the up-market version of the

A Mary Quant design that has not stood the test of time, 1967.

hippies' favourite trouser, the sailors' style originally designed to be pulled off without having to remove their boots. The hippy look was usually home-made with cut-out triangles of denim giving the extra width required. A crazy few went further and ballooned out their bags with velvet and batik inserts known understandably as 'elephant bells'.

Something nasty in the wood, 1970s.

Dishonourable Mentions

Pinstripe jeans

never the twain should meet

27

No Room for Ferrets

Drainpipe trousers

If the 1930s and 1940s were the decades of the Oxford bag and the Zoot suit, then the late 1950s and early 1960s can justly lay claim to being the decades of the drainpipe. Whether you were a Mod or a Rocker, slim strides were the order of the day. Only your old dad wore baggy trousers any more – 12in bottoms were what you wanted.

Rockers topped their skin-tight jeans with black leather jackets, Teddy boys with draped jackets down to their knees. The Mods looked to Italy for their fashion inspiration and were into smooth, shiny suits, all with the slim-legged look. But nothing beat the true drainpipe, the only trouser you have to put on lying down. Even when The Beatles came along and rock turned into pop, the slim trouser still looked great with the Pierre Cardin jackets and floppy hair. But by the end of the 1960s, the

Jiving the night away in retro regulation 'Teddy' boy drains, 1975.

28

With 12in bottoms, only the slimmest could squeeze into 'hip-hugging hipster jeans', 1960s.

More likely to make it small in these Beatles-inspired slim-Jim strides, 1960s.

how to make it big

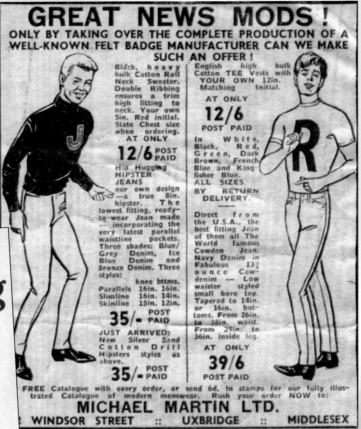

GREAT NEWS MODS !
ONLY BY TAKING OVER THE COMPLETE PRODUCTION OF A WELL-KNOWN FELT BADGE MANUFACTURER CAN WE MAKE SUCH AN OFFER !

Black, heavy bulk Cotton Roll Neck Sweater. Double Ribbing ensures a trim high fitting to neck. Your own 5in. Red initial. State Chest size when ordering.
AT ONLY
12/6 POST PAID

Hip Hugging HIPSTER JEANS our own design —a true 8in. hipster. The lowest fitting, ready-to-wear Jean made — incorporating the very latest parallel waistline pockets. Three shades: Blue/Grey Denim, Ice Blue Denim and Bronze Denim. Three styles:

knee bttms.
Parallels 16in. 16in.
Slimline 16in. 12in.
Skinline 15in. 12in.
35/- POST PAID

JUST ARRIVED: New Silver Sand Cotton Drill Hipsters styles as above.
35/- POST PAID

English high bulk Cotton TEE Vests with YOUR OWN 12in. Matching initial.
AT ONLY
12/6 POST PAID

In White, Black, Red, Green, Dark Brown, French Blue and Kingfisher Blue. ALL SIZES. BY RETURN DELIVERY.

Direct from the U.S.A., the best fitting Jean of them all The World famous Cowden Jean. Navy Denim in Fabulous 13½ ounce Cowdenim — Low waister styled small bore top. Tapered to 14in. or 16in. bottoms. From 26in. to 38in. waist. From 29in. to 36in. inside leg.
AT ONLY
39/6 POST PAID

FREE Catalogue with every order, or send 6d. in stamps for our fully illustrated Catalogue of modern menswear. Rush your order NOW to:
MICHAEL MARTIN LTD.
WINDSOR STREET :: UXBRIDGE :: MIDDLESEX

Long-forgotten Labels
Farahs should never have left the golf course

drainpipe's days were doomed. Flamboyant flares were just round the corner and only heavy metal bands and their fans would carry on clinging to the tightest trousers around – and vice versa.

2

Suits You

Claws out

Catsuits

Worst Women's
6
Fashions

Mamma Mia – classic Abba clobber in blue and lavender Lycra, 1979.

Meow ... catsuits look great on characters out of comics but rarely look good on humans. Originating from Batman's feline jewel thief in the 1940s, it wasn't until the 1960s that the fabric technology was available to create all-in-one suits that clung to every curve. They were a long way from Monsieur Jules Leotard's first attempts in 1859 to design a one-piece suit he could wear for his trapeze performances.

In the space-obsessed 1960s, catsuits were the future. Everyone would be wearing

them on the space stations of the twenty-first century according to TV shows such as *Star Trek* and *Buck Rogers*. From Captain Kirk to Superman, the all-in-one was going to be the space suit of choice.

The most famous wearer in the 1960s was Diana

Rigg when she took over from Honor Blackman as Steed's new sidekick, Emma Peel, in the popular TV series *The Avengers*. Top designer John Bates was brought in to create a strikingly different look via his 'Jean Varon' label. While Blackman had championed the black leather jumpsuit, Rigg's catsuits were even more figure-hugging. With a figure like Rigg's inside them, they became every man's fantasy come true. Great for leaping out of windows but just plain silly for doing the shopping in.

Even Diana Rigg, aka Emma Peel, in 1966 could look ridiculous – why no pixie hat?

Collarless or Clueless

Nehru suits

'The 1971 party man is a far cry from his counterpart a decade ago,' claimed a 1970s trade magazine trying to promote evening wear for men with 'Nehru' styling. There have been occasional cultural cross-overs from foreign countries, but invariably the item looks better on the natives of that country than on fashion-obsessed Westerners. The Nehru jacket was the height of elegance for that eponymous and venerable Indian politician, while Peter Sellers never quite carried off his snakeskin version. But showbiz types loved them: all-round entertainer Sammy Davis Jr claimed to have owned over 200 of these jackets.

Another version that found fame was the low-necked fashion worn by The Beatles in the early 1960s. Spurred on by manager Brian Epstein and inspired by Pierre Cardin, the Fab Four's tailor Dougie Millings came up with their signature style of light grey, black-trimmed, collarless suits worn with the obligatory Beatle boot provided by dance-shoe manufacturers Anello & Davide. The Beatles did not stay with this look for long. Individuality burst out as even The Beatle haircut

Notable/nasty Nicholas Hoogstraten on the way to court, 1968.

32

1960s style of suiting that somehow never quite caught on, 1965.

went the way of all management make-overs. Most infamous wearer of the collarless jacket must surely be Nicholas Hoogstraten, property millionaire and notorious slum landlord, who favoured the 'Nehru' look when he faced criminal charges in Brighton in 1968.

When they ask Sammy about his Nehru suit, he tells them he had it made. And he's not putting them on.

The all-singing, all-dancing Sammy Davis Jnr with his favourite collarless look, 1960s.

33

a JUMP too FAR

Jumpsuits

The jumpsuit was one of the most unflattering garments ever invented. In addition, it was the most difficult piece of clothing to get in and out of, especially at crucial moments. Pity the poor pilots and parachutists who had to wear it. Even when they were not skin-tight, jumpsuits still involved a great deal of unzipping and unbuttoning, stepping in and out of and all for the sake of what? Something that clung in all the wrong places, pretended to be a normal outfit and always made your bum look big.

The king of jumpsuit crime was the King himself, Elvis Presley. Many other rock and pop stars from Abba downwards may have followed in his wake, jumpsuit-wise, but nobody quite tops the cut and the glitz of

Jumping jiminy – it's enough to give you spots before the eyes, 1970.

TV presenter Anneka Rice taking the parachute jumpsuit a pattern too far, 1988.

those 1970s suits that the King wore for his Las Vegas concerts and TV appearances. Designed for him by Bill Belew of the Hollywood-based IC Costume Company, they were elaborate concoctions of vinyl, leather and rhinestones – once seen, never forgotten.

The King in one of his famous jumpsuits made by Hollywood designer Bill Belew, 1975.

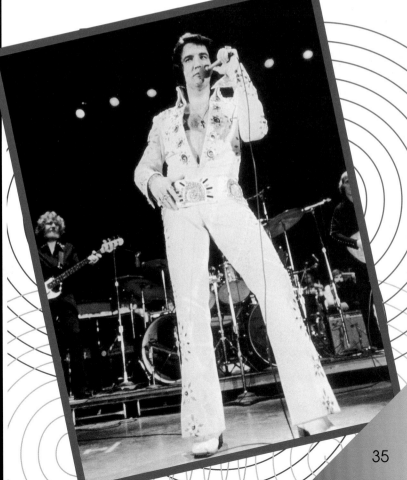

OUT OF AFRICA

Safari suits

Worst Men's 8 Fashions

Someone told him it's a jungle out there, 1970s.

By the 1960s, we may have lost the Empire, but sadly we had not lost that remnant of colonial dressing, the safari suit. There was an element of the 'huntin' and 'fishin' look about it as well. Except that by the 1970s, the safari suit was as far removed from a loch full of trout as it was from a mud bank full of hippos. If ever there was a case for bringing back the classic three-piece suit then this was it. The safari suit did not know quite what it was. It was not a smart suit for the City and it certainly was not a lounging about outfit with all those fussy pockets and the old self-trim belt. What did the safari bwanas put in all those pockets? Yet in the 1970s, guys felt as though they had just stepped out of a James Bond movie wearing one of these outfits.

For the slightly older or more cautious man, this was doing 'casual'. Not for them the hippie or the 'glam rock' look. Just to be a little bit more daring, they put away the dark suit and pretended they had just come 'out of Africa'. And to be really modern, it had to be made out of a synthetic material like Crimplene. Thank goodness, the safari suit had disappeared into the sunset by the 1980s.

There was no escaping the Crimplene look even on safari, 1970s.

WHITE FEVER

White suits

D id anyone wear a white suit before John Travolta in *Saturday Night Fever* in 1978? Did anyone wear a white suit after John was seen strutting his stuff as Tony Manero? Not many. Because who could follow in the footsteps of this man? The album of the film may have sold 20 million copies but only the naffest male would attempt to step into his boogie shoes. You could end up looking more like Lionel Blair than Tony Manero.

But synthetic fabric manufacturer ICI hoped its predictions in the snappily titled 'ICI Fibres and The Crystal Ball of Fashion' were right: 'John Travolta ... and the disco revolution will make their mark on fashion.' After all, Travolta's suit was made from white Dacron, a polyester material with the breathability of a plastic bag, which he wore with a Qiana black nylon shirt. Never heard of Qiana? Not surprising. Designed to be a couture synthetic fabric, when it was used in the Paris salon of couturier Balmain, Qiana

John Travolta – the iconic image for every 1970s disco dancer, 1977.

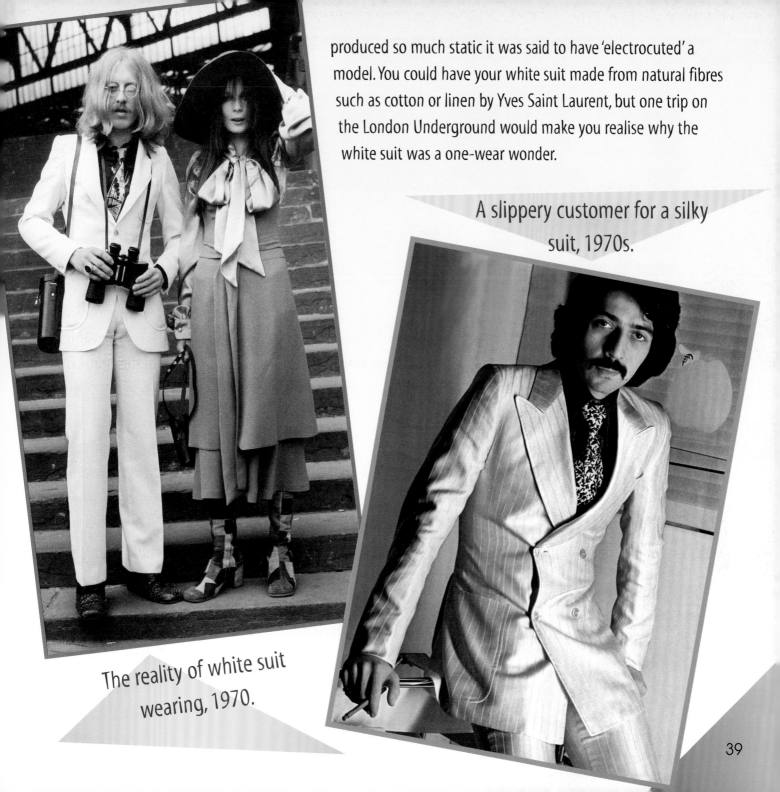

produced so much static it was said to have 'electrocuted' a model. You could have your white suit made from natural fibres such as cotton or linen by Yves Saint Laurent, but one trip on the London Underground would make you realise why the white suit was a one-wear wonder.

A slippery customer for a silky suit, 1970s.

The reality of white suit wearing, 1970.

39

Tracksuits

"What's bright, stylish and soft all over?"

"Us!"

Soft and furry – and that was just the tracksuits, 1980s.

It is hard to imagine life without tracksuits but there was a time when people managed to keep warm on the football pitch or running track with just a woolly jumper. We were a hardier lot in those days. But then along came a revolutionary outfit, stretch knit that did not bag – well, not for the first few hours anyway – warm and comfortable, oh so comfortable. So comfortable that some people never wanted to take them off: doing the shopping, walking the dog, crashing out in front of the television, anywhere and everywhere that had little to do with running tracks but everything to do with easy living.

So the tracksuit turned from a sports garment to a 'leisure' garment. And therein lies the clue. For the first time, people had more leisure time and wanted an alternative to suits, even jeans, and

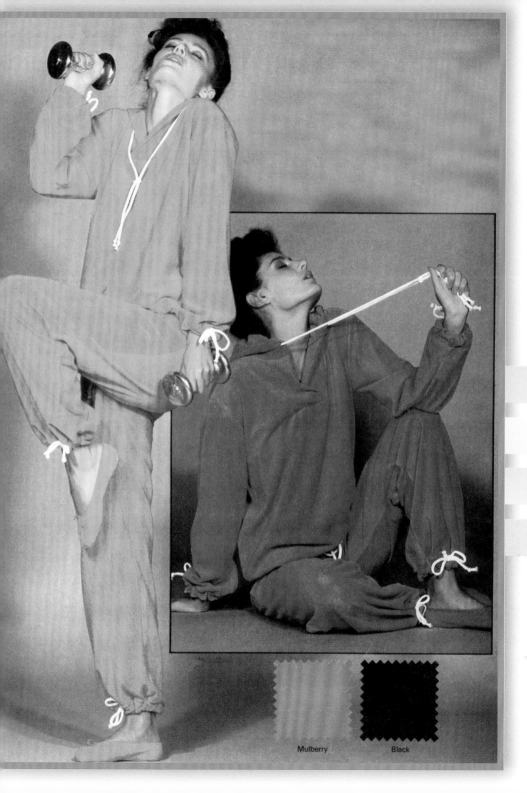

certainly collars and ties. Once a fashion item, there was no stopping the designers from turning sports fashions into street fashions and making millions for the manufacturers. It may never be possible to say goodbye to street sportswear, but the era of those ghastly, unflattering ankle-grabbers is over, thank goodness.

Towelling tracksuit terrors in hideous colours, 1980s.

Mulberry   Black

Shelling Out

Shell suits

Worst Women's 5 Fashions

Own up. Did you ever own a shell suit? Don't deny it – you know, one of those ghastly tracksuits made of shiny, synthetic material. If you did then you are guilty of committing one of the worse fashion sins of the twentieth century according to a recent BBC survey. Shell suits have absolutely no mitigating features. They looked cheap (usually because they were cheap), they were so shiny you could almost see your face in them and they were sometimes even noisy as the shiny fabric rubbed between your legs. And the colours. Was there a shell suit ruling body that

Rod Stewart strutting his stuff in a shell suit shiny enough to see your face in, 1979.

insisted that only the most lurid colours could be used? Probably the worst ever variation was the *Teenage Mutant Hero Turtles* shell suit, too embarrassing to contemplate for anyone over the age of 13.

Yet for far too long, it was considered completely acceptable to wear these monstrosities whether hanging round on street corners or pushing a trolley up the supermarket aisle. This is one fashion that was never going to look retro-cool even in an ironic way – unless of course, you wanted to look like a refugee from *Birds of a Feather* or *Ali G*. Hang your head in shame.

The classic shell suit look for her – guaranteed to look ghastly, 1991.

SYNTHETIC SMELLS

It wasn't just fabrics that were being threatened by a synthetic take over. In 1981, one of the strongest of the new breed of synthetic perfumes arrived in the marketplace. The first perfume to be launched by mail order with scent-impregnated strips as testers, Giorgio Beverly Hills was so strong that restaurants on both sides of the Atlantic banned its wearing so as not to interfere with the culinary experience of fellow diners.

Dishonourable Mentions

White jeans with black boots? Come on!

3

Pure Fabrication

Uncrushable Women

Crimplene for women

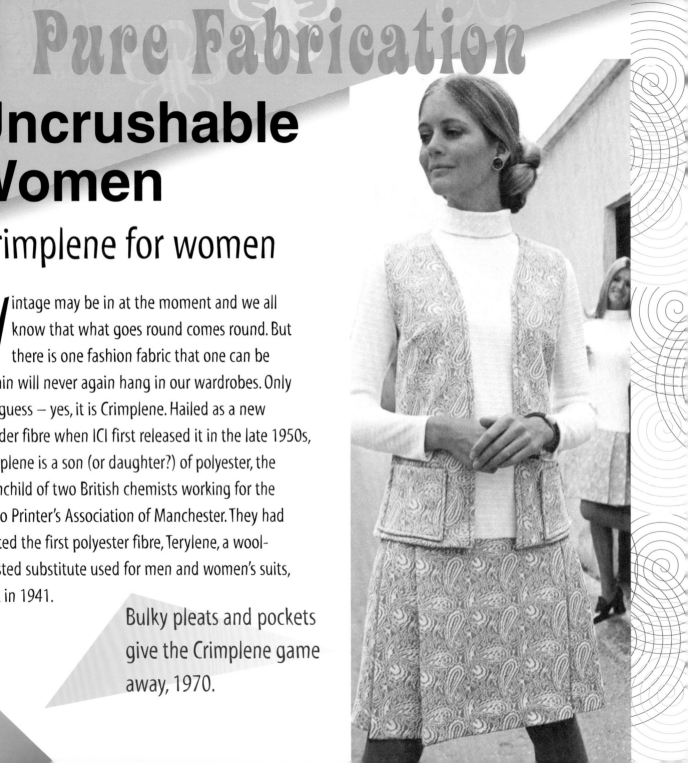

Vintage may be in at the moment and we all know that what goes round comes round. But there is one fashion fabric that one can be certain will never again hang in our wardrobes. Only one guess – yes, it is Crimplene. Hailed as a new wonder fibre when ICI first released it in the late 1950s, Crimplene is a son (or daughter?) of polyester, the brainchild of two British chemists working for the Calico Printer's Association of Manchester. They had created the first polyester fibre, Terylene, a wool-worsted substitute used for men and women's suits, back in 1941.

Bulky pleats and pockets give the Crimplene game away, 1970.

To counteract polyester's rather cold feel, it was 'crimped' to produce a softer fabric, hence Crimplene. This wonder fabric was going to solve all our problems. 'Easycare' was the buzzword – it was washable and did not need any ironing and, in fact, it was not a good idea to iron it since it might have melted with the heat. The fabric was not the only thing that would have melted. Unlike natural fabrics, polyester's breathability was poor. This did not stop manufacturers from producing some of the century's most astoundingly awful outfits in colours and patterns that make leopardskin look tasteful.

Worst fabric for women
CRIMPLENE

Whatever the style, the look of Crimplene was unmistakable, 1970.

Wrinkle-free men

Crimplene for men

What man would not be seduced by the words 'uncrushable' and 'completely washable'? Hardly any, one suspects, especially in the 1960s when the last thing any man had to think about was washing his own clothes. But for the woman in his life, the very thought of such easy-care clothing must have been

The hair matched the synthetic look of the clothes, 1970s.

Crimplene for men

46

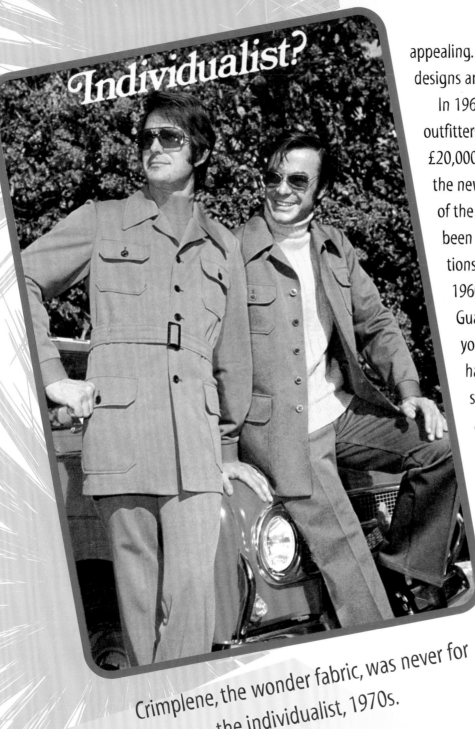

Individualist?

Crimplene, the wonder fabric, was never for the individualist, 1970s.

appealing. Shouldn't that be 'appalling' if these designs are anything to go by?

In 1964, Hepworth's, the High Street men's outfitters, gave the Royal College of Art £20,000 to come up with futuristic designs for the new ICI wonder fabric 'Crimplene'. None of the results survived, but they must have been better than these hideous combinations of those two dreaded words from the 1960s, Crimplene and safari suit. A pair of Guards Leanline 70 trousers may have set you back only £6 19s 6d and they might have been machine washable – but stylish? The stitched-down seams say it all. Any man wearing a Crimplene safari suit would soon have got hot under the collar. No wonder the man in the blue suit is standing with his arm out. He would definitely need to drip dry after wearing one of those all day.

Worst fabric for men CRIMPLENE

Lurid Lurex

Lurex

All that glisters is not gold and all that is shiny is certainly not glamorous. While outfits made from metal clearly had their disadvantages, a metallic yarn that did not tarnish and could be cut, woven, even knitted into any shape seemed like the answer to every woman's prayer, especially for those who longed for evening glamour and sophistication. Plasticised aluminium aka Lurex was just one of the new metallic materials developed in the space-crazy 1960s, which included silver-backed fabrics designed to look like the insulation suits used by astronauts. That was just the effect that men's retailer Cecil Gee went for with his outrageous 'Gee-Man' silver jumpsuit in 1967. This was going to be the future; this was how we were all going to dress in the year 2000 – silver mini skirts and a suit that looked ready to be popped into the oven and roasted for a couple of hours at gas mark 6.

What happened to the shiny silver look? It ended up in the knitting wool

Scratchy and silver, an evening look to be avoided, 1970.

department waiting to be threaded through an evening jumper or woven into some scratchy fabric that only a dowager would think of wearing. Lurex was to evening wear what Babycham was to champagne. Real glamour was never glittery or scratchy and rarely knitted. From silver knitting wools to gold lamé paper taffeta, this was definitely one to be avoided.

Avant-garde, space-age designs never did catch on, 1967.

Wet, Wet, Wet

PVC

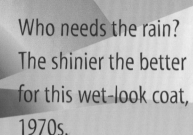

Who needs the rain? The shinier the better for this wet-look coat, 1970s.

How appropriate that the V in PVC stands for vinyl which, as any true music buff knows, is what records (remember them?) were made of. Because the PVC wet-look fabrics really hit the fashion headlines in that *Top of the Pops* era, the 1960s. Polyvinyl chloride had been developed in the 1930s and it quickly became clear that it could be used as a waterproof coating for fabric at a low cost. Its cheapness meant that fashion designers soon took it up as a

50

possible replacement for leather. Unfortunately, early versions cracked in the cold as they stiffened up.

However, once colour was added to the coating, the fun began. Mary Quant produced a 'Wet Look' collection in 1964, but she later admitted that the fabric was a disaster to sew since the seams perforated and tore with the slightest tension. Soon, however, canary yellow and tomato red PVC fabrics were cut into every shape imaginable from catsuits to thigh-high boots and purses to wipe-down dresses. Patterns from snakeskin to floral daisies and animal prints were printed on. Never mind that it was hot and sticky to wear. The fad had passed by the 1970s, even though Jean-Paul Gaultier tried to bring it back to the catwalk in 1996. Today, PVC has a new client base among a more select group: you will find it alongside the rubber and the leather in fetish catalogues – a forty-year journey from M&S to S&M.

No hiding place for this red hunter, 1970s.

51

Feeling Crushed

Crushed velvet and velour

Velvet has been around for centuries, usually seen on the backs of kings or the seats of smart dining chairs. But in the 1960s, new manufacturing techniques meant that thinner, cheaper velvet flooded the fashion fabric market. Still basically a cotton material, once dyed in exotic purples and maroons, it was the perfect accompaniment for hippy cheesecloth tops and hairbands. What man wanted a boring black dress suit when he could have a velvet one made to wear with his patterned shirt and silk neckerchief? The dandy was back. Girls for their part clamoured for Biba's velveteen dresses.

But in the synthetic 1970s, velveteen was too natural – it was hard to wash and it bagged at the knees. What was needed was a new wonder fabric: velour. Velour was modern, made of Celanese Arnel triacetate-and-nylon, or Courtauld's Tricel. Soon you did not need to worry about your velvet looking wrinkled – it was supposed to be like that.

Together with beads and fringed bags, velvet was a key part of the hippy look, 1970.

Cheap velvet imports in crazy colours were highly sought-after, 1960s.

Crushed velvet jersey was everywhere. Soft and stretchy, even tracksuits were being made out of it. Every woman wanted a pair of elastic-waisted crushed velvet evening trousers in the 1980s. They were comfortable, casual and classy – whoops, sorry, never classy.

Synthetic velour brought velvet to the High Street, 1980.

53

What a Stitch-up

Patchwork

Patchwork has been around for centuries, the perfect way to use up old scraps of material to create bedcovers and the like. For clothes before the 1960s? Rarely if ever. But towards the end of that decade, it seemed to hit just the right note with hippy *fashionistas*. It is unlikely they were doing it because they cared about the planet and wanted to recycle their old clothes even in those days. Though dressmaking was a skill still taught to teenage girls in most schools at that time, few would have been bothered to 'cut'n'sew' themselves. But the patchwork craze

BEAUTY PATCHES

TUNIC

TUNIC BACK AND FRONT ALIKE

MATERIALS: 1 oz. Twilley's Bubbly in each of 12 colours; 1 two-oz. ball Stalite; two No. 9 knitting needles.
Measurements: To fit 34 in. bust; length, 31 ins.
Tension: 21 st. square, 3 ins.
Abbreviations: See page 40.
BASIC SQUARE: Work in garter stitch throughout. Cast on 1 st. Inc. 1 st. at beg. of every row up to the number of sts. given in patt. K. 2 tog. at beg. of every row until 1 st. remains. Fasten off.
TO MAKE: Work half of each square in a different colour. Make 24 squares, inc. to 23 sts, 24 inc. to 25 sts. Working centre 4 rows in Stalite make 56 squares inc. to 21 sts.

sts.
→ 23
→ 25

Patchwork wasn't just stitched, it could be knitted into ugly squares as well, 1970s.

KAFTAN EAST

PATCHWORK SKIRT

Style No. 880

Ultra smart wrap-around skirt. Combination of vibrant colours in checks, stripes and plain patches in heavy cotton. Machine washable. To fit all sizes up to 36″ Waist.

£5·95

plus p & p 25p

caught hold not just for pretty cotton materials, which were made up into tops, skirts, shirts and even men's trousers, but for using up old knitting wools and even bits of leather and suede as well. Here was a cheap and cheerful way of getting the leather look just by using all the scraps that were left over. Unfortunately, it just never looks more than it was – pieces of material cobbled together to make a dog's dinner of an outfit. Send it back to the bedspread where it belongs.

The bedspread look was all the rage for happy hippies, 1970s.

KEEP ON RUNNING

The most famous lunchbox, sorry, shorts outfit recently must be sprinter Linford Christie's blue Lycra number famously worn by him at the peak of his career in the mid-1990s. The result of new technology, his suit was made with a double-layered fabric, the inner one, water absorbent, the outer one, water repellent. Now it is standard wear for most serious runners. But, please, keep these shorts on the track not on the street.

Beyond Borg

Artificial sheepskin

In the late 1960s, when all synthetic materials were being hailed as the fabrics of the future, fake furs were everywhere. But in 1970 *Du Pont* Magazine hailed the arrival in the UK of something different: the latest innovation that was being produced by George W. Borg, inventor of synthetic furs, which came to be forever known just as Borg. If you know that it was made from a knitted fabric developed firstly for paint rollers and car-polishing pads, it is easy to see that this was not going to be aimed at a sophisticated luxury market. But the arrival of yet another synthetic material that was supposed to look like soft lambs' coats did get designers very excited. Borg's profits soared to $38 million in 1968 when it sold 13 million metres of fabric in the USA.

Curly and flat, Borg was much easier to handle than earlier shag-pile fake furs and fashion designers loved its fluffy contrast to the shiny and brash materials like PVC. Borg was blatantly fake, not trying to be something it was

All zipped and buttoned up on a cuddly synthetic coat, 1970.

not. It did indeed look like a car polishing pad, you could pop it in the washing machine – although within days it looked as though it had been polishing a car again. Since the arrival of fleece, nowadays you hardly even find it on the garage forecourt.

SPLASHING OUT

Knitted bathing costumes may be in the past but plenty of us wish that skin-tight Speedos for men had gone that way as well. Ever since the arrival of Lastex from the USA in the 1950s, swimming costumes have been able to retain their cling. Some were so tight they were like elastic corsets. In the 1970s, women went cotton and crochet mad, but sadly men dived into embarrassingly brief briefs in lurid colours and even worse patterns. Top swimwear manufacturers such as Jantzen and Speedo competed to produce men's swimwear so small that it should not have left the changing room. Janzten proudly proclaimed it owned the beach with its 'form-fitting, stretch swimwear we call Bodyworks'. Yet somehow it will always be the word 'Speedos' that will conjure up images of beach bodies best forgotten. By the 1990s, quick-drying beach shorts hung round young men's hips while super-swimmers covered up with go-faster bodysuits.

Shiny meets shaggy in this raincoat
– just don't get it wet, 1970.

4

Frightful Frocks & Silly Skirts

Knitted Nightmares

Knitted dresses

Worst Women's 10 Fashions

With the arrival of an avalanche of artificial yarns in the 1960s, manufacturers went into overdrive to come up with designs to use them for. Not that knitted dresses were that new. There had been a vogue for knitted suits and costumes in the 1920s and then they vanished again as the 1930s version of power shoulders arrived.

Technology to mass-produce knitted outfits appeared in the 1960s.

A crêpe wool, knitted nightmare dress, 1970s.

Over seven years, Courtaulds invested £400 million in acquisitions, expansions and upgrades, particularly of knitted jersey – that is as a knitted fabric, not a garment. Chain stores up and down the country were selling jersey dresses that were supposed to be both comfortable and fashionable. Alarm bells should have been ringing: 'comfortable' and 'fashionable' are words that rarely go together and certainly not in this case.

In reality these dresses clung to all the wrong bits, 1970s.

These dresses were comfortable because they clung, and clinging jersey dresses show every bulge, every spare tyre and every bra and panty line. That did not stop millions of women, especially of a size who should have known better, wearing one of the most boring and unflattering fashions of the 1960s. If you were 16, it made you look 60, and if you were 60, it made you look sad. Like anything with an elasticated waist (think coach parties and printed pink pleats), this was a slow-burner that eventually died out.

Going to Great Lengths

Maxi skirts

Everything that goes up must come down the saying goes. But the extremes that skirt lengths went to in the early 1970s were different to other fashion trends. Rumour had it that this fashion was started by the fabric manufacturers, naturally. They were getting desperate about the small amounts of material that were needed to make miniskirts. First they encouraged production of maxi-coats, jolly useful for a mini-skirted girl in the cold winter with next to nothing between her nether regions and the howling wind; looked great with long boots as well. Then maxi skirts were thrust into the shops in an effort to get girls to part with their beloved mini and cover up with yards and yards of material.

Knee-length was not good enough, it had to be ankle-length or even better down to the ground. Never mind that running for a bus now became a major obstacle course;

never mind that going on an escalator now involved facing a minefield of potential dangers. The main thing was that women had to replace their wardrobes with new and completely different length clothes to keep abreast of the latest styles.

The trouble was that women did not fall for it. This was the age of the feminist, of bra-burning and fights for equality. Women had not got this far to go back to all the restrictions that long skirts imposed on their lifestyles. So a compromise was reached. Skirts crept up to mid-calf and there were hot pants for those who dared. Skirt lengths never went to such dramatic sweeps of change again.

Ankle to neck coverage was encouraged by fabric makers, 1970.

Wrap-round maxi skirts used even more fabric to the delight of makers, 1970s.

Flower Power

Flowery dresses

'If you're going to San Francisco, be sure to wear a flower in your hair,' went the song, but in the early 1970s, the hippie movement had lost its influence and fashion had been taken over by a more commercial floral feel. Laura Ashley was the name on everyone's lips. For the first time for decades, a pretty, feminine look was being commercially produced and by 1979, the company had a turnover of £25 million worldwide.

This was no hippie style, however; it was all cottons and lace, layers and flounces. Suddenly Liberty prints weren't just for little

Flowers and floppy hats were popping up everywhere, 1972.

62

girls' smocks, they were suitable for big sisters' dresses as well. To add to this, you had to have a big floppy hat with daisies sewn on. Now this look may have been great when you were 14, but on a 34-year-old woman it never looked quite right. Fashion is notoriously fickle and once the power-crazed 1980s arrived, the little-girl look was definitely over. Laura Ashley's profits slowly withered away until an Asian company bent on rebranding took it over in 1998. While we may still want daisies on our duvets, few women want a dress that made them look like a herbaceous border.

No escaping flowers and flares in the mid-1970s, 1974.

Krafty Kaftans

Kaftans

Peace, love, marijuana – all part of the hippie look that came out of San Francisco from 1965 onwards. This was the era of the rock festival, of Woodstock in 1969 and Reading, of flower power and psychedelia. It did not take long for style icons The Beatles to dump their look-alike suits and Chelsea boots for a less obviously commercial effect – beads, long hair and the kaftan all arrived in London just as The Beatles became involved with the 'spiritual' side of this new movement.

By the time of the 'Summer of Love' in 1967, it was the height of chic to reject the synthetic fabrics that manufacturers were producing by the ton. There was even a hippie fashion show in London in 1967 with designer Michael Rainey showing off djellabas, Moroccan hooded kaftans, all made from cool, natural fabrics. But this was not mainstream fashion. You could not

Was this the way to San Francisco in 1970 – or the Isle of Wight pop festival?

wear the 'turn on, drop out' clothes you had picked up on your way back from India or Africa to the office. Headbands and beads, body paint and 'Jesus' sandals all belonged to a brief period of fashion history that those who were there probably can't remember. Life had moved on to a psychedelic period of frocked jackets from boutiques such as 'I Was Lord Kitchener's Valet' and 'Granny Takes a Trip'.

The hippie look was never the height of fashion, 1969.

Power to the Shoulders

Padded shoulders

Worst Women's
2
Fashions

Back in the 1980s, women everywhere stuffed their blouses and sweaters with shoulder pads that made them look like members of an American football team. American soaps were to blame: fashion leaders such as Linda Gray, aka Sue Ellen Ewing in *Dallas*, and Joan Collins and Linda Evans, aka Alexis Carrington and Krystle

TV game-show host Debbie Greenwood squares up to the camera, 1988.

SCENT OF FAME

The 1980s saw the arrival of celebrity fragrances which on the whole failed miserably. Most people just saw this as an attempt for the celebrities concerned to earn 'loadsamoney'. Forever Krystle, a scented evocation of the fictional icon of Krystle Carrington, a supposedly sympathetic *Dynasty* character, was just such a flop and quickly disappeared.

in *Dynasty*, went to the extremes on their TV shows and millions followed in their wake.

Shoulder pads of all shapes and sizes were an essential part of every woman's wardrobe in the 1980s. There were chopped-off white ones for big blouses, curved Velcro-ed ones for jumpers, even double-flapped ones to slip under the bra strap just in case. No outfit was complete without padding. The message was clear: we fought the feminist fight in the 1970s, now we want to show you who is boss but stay sexy at the same time. Power dressing was supposed to affirm women's new-found strength. But when the financial bubble burst at the end of the 1980s, such aggressively 'in-your-face' dressing suddenly looked out of place. All you could hear was ripping as pad after pad was torn out and a relaxed *á la* Armani look took over. It says it all that in

2004 the Yellow Pages directory removed shoulder pad manufacturers as a category – not enough suppliers.

Joan Collins – queen of runway shoulders, 1984.

FASHION FACTS With the development of new synthetics, cotton's share of the world fibre market dropped from 75 per cent in 1940–1 to 49 per cent by 1976–7.

all puffed up

Puffball skirts

Absolutely fabulous he may have been in the eyes of *Absolutely Fabulous* Eddie and Patsy, but can we forgive Christian Lacroix for claiming responsibility for producing one of the silliest skirts since the crinoline? The bouffant or 'puff ball' dress that he first showed in 1986 caused a sensation. Love it or hate it, it has stuck in the mind as one of the shapes of the 1980s. But was he really the first to think of the idea? He was certainly the first to put one into a couture Paris show, but back in the early 1960s, black-eyed singer Dusty Springfield was seen wearing something suspiciously like it.

By the end of the 1980s, there were grown-up and teeny-bopper versions if you had the front to wear them. Remember Pepsi & Shirley? No? Shame on you. They were the bubbly backing singers to Wham! How could you forget? Least of all Pepsi's puffball skirts, petticoats and knee-high socks: a look that every 12-year-old wanted to copy – and did. So, unfortunately, did Sarah, Duchess of York. Do not get these skirts confused with ra-ra skirts, another favourite with 12-year-olds then and

One of Sarah, Duchess of York's many early fashion *faux pas*, 1987.

now. Ra-ras, mini minis with frills like a shrunken Spanish dancer's dress, will be with us for a bit longer: only make sure you are not old enough to drive a car if you're thinking of wearing one.

Pepsi & Shirley, better remembered for their skirts than their singing, 1987.

In the Dolmans

Batwing sleeves

Look what happened when you wore enormous shoulder pads, your sleeves started to sag. Well, they certainly did in the 1980s when the batwing sleeve was briefly all the rage. The batwing, or Dolman style of sleeve, had been around since the Middle Ages (let's face it, there have not been any completely new fashion ideas for centuries – surely the toga is set for a revival?) and it competed against the shoulder pad for the silliest shoulder shape.

Manufacturers loved this style – easy to cut, easy to sew, no darts, no fitting, one size fitted all. Well, yes, but then so does a potato sack – and that is what anything with batwing sleeves tended to resemble. Sadly often worn by women who could not cope with the clinched-in waists that the power shoulder outfits required, they usually ended up looking as broad as they were tall. We

Actress Leslie Ash showing off her batwings, 1987.

all know what chicken-leg arms are like on women of a certain age who should know better. The Dolman sleeve was the fabric version of that flabby arm and should have been banished back to the battery factory where it came from.

Washable it may have been, but this jersey cover-up flattered no one, 1980s.

ROYAL FASHION

HM The Queen has always been keen to wear clothes and hats that allow her to stand out in a crowd, but this has twice earned Her Majesty a place on the USA's Worst Dressed Women in the World list. Unfortunately, chic her style isn't. Just like her mother before her, Queen Elizabeth sticks to what she likes and leaves the experimentation to her grand-daughter Zara Phillips, whose pierced tongue was thankfully a short-lived fad. Zara's mother, Princess Anne, is renowned for hanging on to her clothes for decades and recycling outfits she wore twenty years before. In 1999 she dusted off an evening gown she had first been seen wearing in 1973 when Gary Glitter was Top of the Pops. Royal retro-chic? Not quite.

MEN'S CRIMES AGAINST FASHION | Towelling socks | never, never, never

5

Flop of the Tops

Belt up!

Men's belted waistcoats

25-jewel calendar watch
59.95

Did knitwear designers really expect men to wear these 1970s grandad versions of the tank top? Obviously they did. After all, the Professor Higgins cardigan as seen in *My Fair Lady* had been a huge fashion hit just a few years before in the early 1960s. But nothing with a knitted belt has ever been fashionable.

As every girl knows, a knitted belt gives you no support and just cuts across the most

MEN'S CRIMES AGAINST FASHION | Hawaiian shirts | only DJs can get away with them

difficult part of the body, style-wise, the tum. But just for a while in the early 1970s, men really wore these belted knitted waistcoats. They were something of a leftover from the hippy fashions for long velvet waistcoats – this was the ugly High Street knitted version. Luckily it did not last too long. The bad news: it shrank pretty quickly to become one of the true style horrors of the 1970s – the tank top.

Pre-tank tops, the granddad look had plenty of appeal, 1970.

Suave synthetics made for a model look which included knitted trousers, 1970s.

You can make a fantastic break in THREE PIECE SETS at Man at C&A.
Sweater, tunic and flare-bottomed trousers. Full-stretch freedom knitted Orlon/Antron. Colour combinations black/... black/orange... Sizes 36 to 40... you might...

What a Boob!

Boob tubes

Although we should thank Du Pont, the inventors of Lycra, for many things, the boob tube is not one of them. But at the start of the 1980s, every girl who had boobs had to have a tube or two. However, quite a few boobless girls refused to be tubeless. Which was unfortunate, because you really needed a bust for the thing to stay up. The tighter the tube the more it wanted to migrate down to your waist unless you had a little something to provide support. But if you did have something to keep it up, it did that no favours either, squashing your bosom into a shapeless sausage – large or small, depending on your cup size.

It is one thing to wear a boob tube on the beach lying on a lounger all day but it is hardly disco wear. Yet in the early 1980s, sequinned boob tubes were essential club wear despite the risk of revealing all in the middle of throwing your arms in the air. Like the other great 1980s top, the 'body' – whose poppers came open when you did not want them to and stayed firmly shut when you did – the boob tube should have been a one-summer wonder, but stayed around just a bit too long.

Charlie's Angel Jaclyn Smith didn't dare lift her arms in her boob tube, 1980.

The glitzier the better for silly sequinned evening wear, 1981.

The 1980s summer must-have – a cotton/Lycra boob tube, hopefully non-slip, 1980.

The Tanks Roll in

Men's tank tops

Worst Men's
4
Fashions

Looking more like a shrunken vest than a jumper, the tank top for men is one of the greatest crimes against men's fashion in the last century. Knitted waistcoats and vests had been around since the 1930s when the home knitting boom inspired thousands of wives and mothers to take up

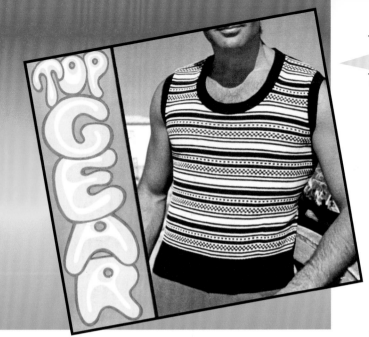

TOP GEAR

The more colour and pattern the better for these macho tank tops, 1970s.

their needles and knit a little something. These were worn under a jacket to replace the more formal fabric waistcoat that came with a three-piece suit. But these were a looser style and usually v-necked and were as popular in the suburbs as a pipe and slippers.

By the early 1970s everything was getting tighter and smaller. Trousers may have had flared bottoms,

Marty Kristian of The New Seekers sported his essential trendy credentials – low-cut tank top, long hair and zip-fly flares, 1972.

but their tops left little to the imagination. High-waisted trousers, collars big and round like a labrador's tongue, hair down to the shoulders if you were daring enough, the tank top completed the quintessential 1970s look. Chief culprit? Where to start? Noel Edmonds knows he cannot avoid being called Tank Top King of Saturday morning television. *Swap Shop* memories come flooding back. Now thankfully worn only by geeky academic types.

MEN'S CRIMES AGAINST FASHION   Ray-Ban glasses   no longer the coolest guy in town

KNIT ONE

Girls' tank tops

It cannot be denied any longer. While everyone has a big laugh about men and their tank tops in the 1970s, women have got to admit that the girls were just as guilty of wearing them. Well, maybe not quite so guilty because tank tops did not look as silly on girls as they did on men – but almost.

The sad thing is that we probably got our mums to knit them for us. It was the perfect way to use up a few odd balls of wool left over from

Who wouldn't be upset wearing clothes like these, 1975.

granny's jumper. And it was easy too – no sleeves to attach, no buttonholes. In fact, girls' tank tops may have been the last fashion item that your mum could make you and you would not get laughed at – back in the 1970s anyway. Because, while almost every other fashion has gone and come back again, it is a pretty safe bet that there is as much chance of seeing tank tops come back as there is of seeing a footballer in a skirt. Oh dear …

Best-forgotten fashions
Champion sweatshirts
never a match for the big boys
of sportswear

Knit one, purl one, any scrap of wool would do as long as it was colourful, 1970s.

Don't get Shirty

Men's patterned shirts

Where did all the white shirts go in the 1960s? Were any actually made and bought? Because it seems that every shirt worn at this time was in a yet more hideous colour and more garish pattern than the last one. In the 1930s, the Men's Dress Reform Party had tried and failed to get men to wear more colourful shirts. Although plenty would have liked to, they were too much associated with the despised 'dandy' and 'queer' scene. But by the 1960s, the dandy was back as a central part of the swinging London set.

Leading London designers David Mlinaric and Tom Gilbey both claim credit for being the first to sew frills to the front of shirts in the

Steptoe's dad Wilfred Brambell showing he was as groovy as the next guy, 1971.

mid-1960s, thus starting a fashion that went from the disco to the dinner-and-dance circuit. Gilbey designed outfits for top pop group The Kinks, having decided that their long hair was just right for a

Regency fop look. Pop stars like Jeff Beck of The Yardbirds and Ronnie Lane of The Small Faces led the way on the patterned shirt front. King of the Mods, Lane reputedly bought up the whole stock of Carnaby Street fashion Mecca shop Lord John because he did not want to see anyone else wearing them.

From an original design by legendary designer Tommy Nutter, 1970s.

IF YOUR DATE SAYS GOODNIGHT WITH A HANDSHAKE,

BETTER JOIN THE CLUB.

Win her with flowers—the colorful ones on this sport knit. The pattern is ours alone. 100% Arnel® triacetate knit. About $13.50. Career Club Shirt Co., Inc., 350 Fifth Avenue, New York 10001 · 1974.

CAREER CLUB KNITS

Celanese® Arnel®

Where-To-Buy-It? Use REACTS Card—Page 59.

Jeff Beck, lead guitarist with 1960s R & B group The Yardbirds, sports a flowered shirt from Carnaby Street's John Stephen, 1966.

Hot Under the Collar

Men's big collars

It hardly seems possible that the dog's tongue collar was ever anything other than an awful 1970s fashion cliché, but when Mick Jagger married Bianca in 1971, what was he wearing? Yes, unbelievably, the King of Cool himself wore a patterned shirt with a collar so round and long it would not have disgraced Noel Edmonds on *Swap Shop*. By the mid-1970s, this monster collar was round every male neck in the country, bedecked with enormously wide and long 'kipper' ties.

Which came first? The kipper tie or the long round collar? It has got to be the ties: those involved in fashion evolution would have decreed that smaller (and, it has to be said, less silly) collars would have looked wrong with such a big tie. Really? You never saw the Duke of Windsor wearing such a stupid collar shape even though he loved a big tie. But it was not just the shirt collar you needed to look the part in the

mid-1970s, it was the whole ensemble that brings tears to the eyes: the flared and fitted polyester suit with lapels like landing strips, the platform shoes, the long hair and the pièce de résistance, the patterned shirt with the silly droopy collar.

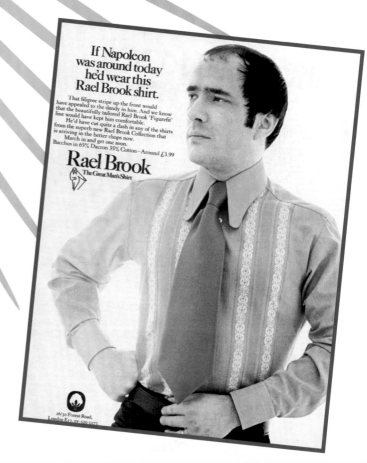

Fancy lace stripes were not just for evening wear, 1970s.

82

Arnold Palmer

takes on the print!

Arnold Palmer trimfit shirts in polyester/cotton.

	Collar sizes	To fit waist
D AC542 BLUE	14	28/30
E AC549 CREAM	14½	30/32
F AC556 BROWN	15	32/34
G AC563 LILAC	15½	34/36
Shirts £2·75 (each)	16	36/38
20 wks 14p	16½	38/40
State collar size		

OUTSTANDING VALUE

£2·75 EACH

Dedicated follower – and leader – of fashion, Mick Jagger marrying Bianca, 1971.

Ace golfer Arnold Palmer was the unlikely label on these very British shirts, 1970s.

SMELLY MEN

Brut aftershave for men was launched in 1963 and in commercial terms was a huge success. But, although rated as one of the most memorable advertising campaigns of the 1970s when world heavyweight boxing championship contender Henry Cooper encouraged previously perfume-shy men to 'splash it all over', *Brut* was such an instantly recognisable fragrance with its sweet, ambery odour, that it was quickly ridiculed. By the 1980s and 1990s, with fading sports stars such as Kevin Keegan and Paul 'Gazza' Gascoigne doing the promotion, its fate was sealed. Now just a whiff brings back memories of platforms and flares. At least *Brut* is remembered, unlike one of its imitators, *Pub Cologne for Men*. Marketed in a rum-barrel-shaped bottle with instantly forgettable tag line, 'Pub for Men uncorks the lusty life', it not surprisingly failed to make a dent in the aftershave market.

Tied up in a Bow

Pussy-cat bows

We are often told we have got a lot to thank former Prime Minister Margaret Thatcher for: cracking down on the unions, defending the Falklands, promoting the big-bow blouse. Hang on a minute. Lady Thatcher, a fashion icon? This doesn't quite ring true. We know she shopped at High Street giant Marks & Spencer and Regent Street's Aquascutum, but they were hardly the cutting edge of street fashion.

The perfect example of 1970s buttoned-up femininity, 1970.

But that was the whole point. When Lady T came to power and had her make-over – teeth, hair, make-up and lower voice – she also went for a distinct look in the way she dressed. She never needed power shoulders (we all knew where the power lay), instead she opted for the Tunbridge Wells school of dressing – smart, tailored suits with kitten-bow blouses, modesty personified, high-buttoned up to the neck. Queen Elizabeth may make it regularly on to Blackwell's

Best-forgotten Fashions
Fruit of the Loom t-shirts
the little logo that was everywhere

Synthetic fabrics were perfect for the drip-dry look, 1970.

Margaret Thatcher leading the fashion trail in floppy bow blouses, 1975.

Worst Dressed Women in the World list, but, in fact, it is the Thatcher look that is more dangerous. Even Diana, Princess of Wales, tried it in her demure days. Sorry, but demure is dead. Big bows have bowed out, thank goodness.

Geometrical Sweaters

Men's jumpers

Knitwear sets in colours to make you wince, 1970.

It is a phenomenon that women will never quite understand, but there is no doubt that many men take what seems to be the most inexplicable pleasure in holding on to their favourite jumpers until the bitter end: that being either when it falls apart or when someone manages to smuggle it out in the charity shop bag. Almost invariably this prized jumper will be hideous because men of a certain age seem to suffer from a form of colour blindness that blots out revolting colours and patterns.

It would be easy to blame 1970s crooner Val Doonican. Every Saturday night for years he invited us folk into his living-room complete with rocking chair, guitar and a myriad array of cringe-making sweaters to listen to such gems as 'Scarlet Ribbons' and 'Walk Tall'.

But that would be a little unfair. In the 1960s, synthetic-yarn manufacturers had started mass-producing outlandish patterns that just would not have been feasible with

Best-forgotten Fashions
Global Hypercolour t-shirts
playground fun for 5 minutes

Mr Smooth himself, Val Doonican, cosy in a comfy jumper, 1989.

What a lucky man to have this made for him, 1969.

natural woollen or cotton yarns. Menswear shops were flooded with cheap, washable designs that nowadays you hardly even see on a golf course, that bastion of poor taste. Not only were they cheap, they were virtually indestructible as well. For these reasons many still lurk in the back of British men's wardrobes, lovingly brought out for a weekend's gardening or decorating.

6 Show a Leg

Too Hot to Handle

Hot pants

Worst Women's 8 Fashions

Best-forgotten Fashions
Hard Rock Café t-shirts
bought the burger, bought the t-shirt along with millions of others

In the early 1970s, they were hot and, yes, they were like pants. And they also brought enormous pleasure to thousands of men who suddenly developed a passionate interest in pop music as every week luscious Babs, Dee Dee, Cherry and co. of Pan's People gyrated across TV screens in *Top of the Pops* in ever briefer hot pants. In offices across the country, men held their breath as secretaries bent over to retrieve 'accidentally' dropped envelopes. Hard on the heels of the mini, hot pants – a phrase purportedly coined by American fashion bible *Women's Wear Daily* in 1970 – have come to symbolise the shock of the sexy in the 1970s. One American airline introduced them as part of the uniform for its stewardesses, and even Royal Ascot

Even a general election couldn't dampen the spirits of these unlikely Tory canvassers, 1971.

allegedly allowed them if the 'general effect' was satisfactory. Unfortunately, there were some pretty ghastly variations in velvet that must have added at least 3in to the hips. The women inside them should have known better. This was a fun fashion for the very young and slim, not the young at heart. Yet when Elizabeth Taylor and Richard Burton arrived at Heathrow Airport in 1971, it is clear who wore the trousers in their relationship. When you're 5ft nothing, curvaceous and pushing 40, then, sorry, hot pants should have been a no-no.

Little Miss Lulu in hot pant horrors – but only just, 1971.

Elizabeth Taylor showing off her *chutzpah*, 1971.

A Short Trip to Bermuda

Bermuda shorts

Worst Men's 9 Fashions

While mystery surrounds the Bermuda Triangle, no mystery surrounds the origins of Bermuda shorts. Early in the twentieth century, British servicemen abroad cut off the bottom half of their formal trousers to help cope with the heat. Not the baggy Boy Scout look. London tailors were soon producing pure linen adaptations for the forces abroad. Only one country adopted them for its national dress. In Bermuda, they can be worn for any formal occasion, including evening events and legislative meetings just as long as they are 3in above the knee.

The problems began when they were taken up in the USA in the 1950s. Designs appeared in crazy colours and plaid patterns – not at all what the staid Bermudians had in mind. A slim man can look good in almost anything, but checked Bermuda shorts test this principle beyond its breaking point. And the rear view of a more substantial man in these could haunt one for days after even the briefest sighting.

Designs by Schwartzmann trying to tempt men into Terylene, 1967.

The 1980s variation was the cut-off jeans look. Not nearly so smart, but just the thing to do with that shrunken pair of jeans. Fraying and slashes completed the transformation from tropical formal wear to savvy street style. By the 1990s, the formal Bermuda short was dead and buried. Shorts just got longer and longer, and baggier and baggier. Surf-style, quick-drying pants from names like Quiksilver and Billabong show where the influence was coming from. The patterns may be Hawaiian, but Aussie surf rules.

Spoilt for choice – a line-up of Bermuda-clad legs, 1960s.

Caught Short
Shorts suits for men

Short history lesson: in the 1930s, a group called the Men's Dress Reform Party tried to get the man in the street to ditch the traditional three-piece suit in favour of wearing shorts all the time – for work, for play and, most hilariously, in place of his dress clothes for the evening. Now here's a surprise. It failed dismally. The average man is reluctant enough to show his knees on a beach, let alone in an office, and certainly never in a dance hall. So what were designers thinking of in the 1960s and 1970s when they tried to resurrect these ideas? Did they really think that they stood a chance of getting men to dispense with the dignity that long trousers gave them for an opportunity to be laughed at? Yet in

Two of top designer Tom Gilbey's less successful ideas for the London man, 1970.

Even designer to HM the Queen Hardy Amies thought shorts might be the way forward, 1966.

An own goal for Paul 'Gazza' Gascoigne's taste in leg wear, 1992.

1966 and 1970 respectively, top British menswear designers Hardy Amies and Tom Gilbey tried to do just that.

Will they never learn that men's legs, even with knee-length socks on, are just not something to be seen except on holiday, under sufferance and preferably tanned? Even then you have only got to look at what happened to Bermuda shorts to wonder if anything above the knee is a good idea for men.

Knickerbocker Glories

What is it about knickerbockers that make them seem so inherently wrong on women? Is it the silly name? No, surely it is the way they look. This is not the principle-boy style, tight breeches in thigh-slapping satin. This is not the plus-four look with its baggy bottoms and usually baggy backside. No, knickerbockers are basically cut-off trousers designed to finish at boot-top level and flounce a little over the top. Which is fine if you are a Royalist cavalier in the mid-seventeenth

Knickerbockers were never the same after Abba's Agnetha Fältskog wore them, 1975.

century, but less amusing if you are a woman in the late twentieth century.

Leg lengths differed and knickerbockers rarely flattered. The worst offenders were undoubtedly Agnetha and Frida of pop group Abba: they took knickerbocker-wearing to a new low with the white satin outfits they wore in the 1970s.

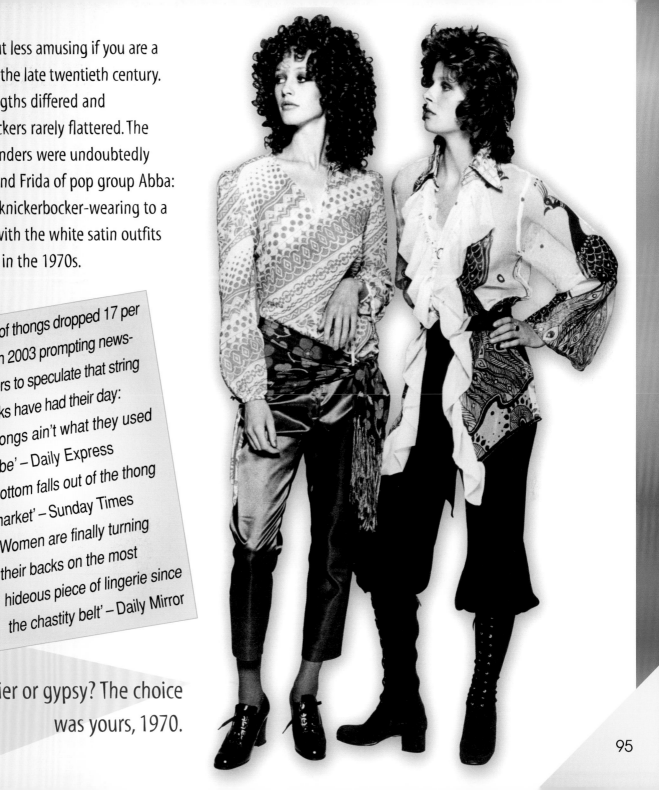

Cavalier or gypsy? The choice was yours, 1970.

Leggings

Elastane, better known as Lycra, the miracle fibre that can now be woven into virtually any fabric and dyed the same colour, was trademarked by Du Pont in 1959. But it was not until the 1980s that its true potential was seen and understood: potential to put every woman under 50 (or who saw herself as still under 50) into skin-tight leggings and pants safe in the knowledge that they would not bag in the knees by mid-afternoon.

In 1987, British designer Georgina Godley produced Lycra leggings that put 'women in what were in effect, tights'. This was just what was needed – comfort clothes to be worn in the gym and home on the streets afterwards. Who needed a girdle or a corset when your leggings could do the job for you? Only the problem was that it often didn't. And the VPL – the visible panty line – came into its own since these bottoms left little to the

Rod Stewart should have known this was not a look for a man, on stage or off, 1979.

A royal redhead who has never looked back since she joined Weight Watchers, 1992.

A sporty look that was too often seen on the streets, 1989.

imagination. In 1996, Marks & Spencer sold £80 million worth of Lycra-based garments. Cheaper versions of leggings with low elastane content bought from market stalls did not have Lycra's exceptional holding power. Sadly, for many overweight women leggings and an outsized sweatshirt became the leisure outfit of choice.

To Top it All

A Shaggy Coat Story — Afghan coats

In the late 1960s when the temperatures dropped, out came the shaggy Afghan coat which was probably claimed to have been bought somewhere along the hippie trail to Kathmandu. Shaggy – and usually smelly, too. Journalist Sue Arnold remembers bringing hers back in the 1970s. 'There [was] an awful smell in the hall ... almost as if something had died and gone rotten.' Her glamorous snow-white embroidered sheepskin smelled, Arnold claimed, 'as if the sheep wasn't dead, just badly wounded, and

The commercial coat never had quite the cachet of the one bought on the Silk Road, 1970s.

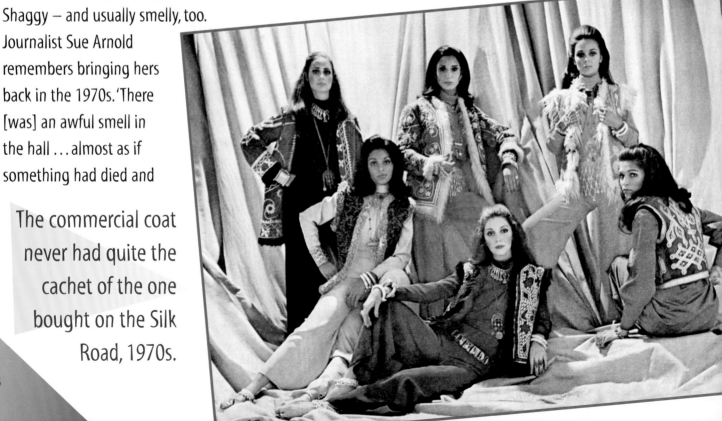

needing its bandages changed ... [making] an open sewer in a Moroccan soukh [pass] as Chanel No. 5.'

Although Afghan coats were indestructible, extremely heavy and usually filthy, some people were loath to get rid of them – or if they did later regretted it. In 2001, Becky Wilkinson, 47, bought back the Afghan coat she sold in the 1970s after seeing it at a jumble sale for £1. Most instantly iconic wearer is probably 'Wolfie' Smith, played by Robert Lindsay and a hero to all followers of the Tooting Popular Front, with his Afghan coat, commando beret and guitar strung over his shoulder back in the early 1980s sitcom *Citizen Smith*.

Who needs to go to Afghanistan? Cheap imports flooded the London markets, 1970s.

For the authentic look, the Afghan had to be ripped and smelly to be hip, 1974.

Don't Parka There!

Parka jackets

What the leather jacket was to the Rocker, the parka was to the Mod. The original 1950s Mods were modernists who were into the music of the Modern Jazz Quartet (as opposed to folk, rock or trad jazz) and related to Italy for its sharp fashions, France for its music and movies. They were a world away from the Mods of the mid-1960s, scooting down to Southend, fox-tails flying from their aerials, wearing, as style specialist Ted Polhemus said, 'grubby parkas festooned with badges worn by kids who knew The Who's lyrics by heart but had never even heard of the MJQ'.

Unfortunately, the cheap high street version of the parka was here to stay. Trimmed with fake fur, it became a toned-down version of the knee-length Mod version, sober enough for any sensible man to wear. Then the stylists got hold of the parka and produced the snorkel jacket. More fake fur, shinier fabrics, knitted cuffs and more bum-freezer styling produced one of the least flattering jackets any man could hope to wear.

In the 1990s, Liam Gallagher wore a long parka in the Oasis video for 'Do Y'Know What I Mean'. Within days, West End shops had sold out of this odd-looking coat and army surplus stores were being scoured for the latest rock look.

Parka Casual Coat
- Fantastic value
- Quilt lining
- Fur-trimmed hood
- Proofed cotton outer cloth.
- Sponge clean.

Parka jackets were a catalogue favourite, 1970s.

100

Fake fur and silver coatings – and a cold bum not for the reticent, 1970s.

Where it all started – a parka parade in Brighton, 1964.

Best-forgotten Fashions
Barbour jackets
only for a Countryside Alliance march

Piling it on

Fake fur coats

Worst Men's 7 Fashions

Fun fake furs from the 1970s fooled no one.

In the 1960s, when everything fake was fun and artificial fabrics were hailed as the future for fashion, it was not long before some clever chemist came up with a fluffy fake fur that was going to bring the warmth and comfort of a real fur coat within the reach of everyone. In the 1950s, circular knitting machines had been adapted to make a pile fabric from synthetic fibres. Horrifically, early fun fur fabrics had very poor flame resistance and at the least would melt when in contact with even a cigarette butt. By 1970, the trade welcomed a flame retardant version, Ribbonfil, which was a filament rayon yarn used for pile fabrics.

These coats were not meant to fool anyone into thinking that they were the real thing. Fake was fine –

or was it? In the 1970s, when it was still OK to wear the real thing, anything else looked cheap and nasty. Although synthetic furs were produced that were supposed to imitate ermine, chinchilla, and mink, with names like 'Persiana – the beauty of Persian lamb ... created from soft, curled nylon', or 'Candaseal – ultra-soft acrylic ... with the look and feel of seal', they kidded no one. Even the anti-fur trend of the 1980s and 1990s produced only a small upturn in sales of fakes despite cool images of Andy Warhol and Lou Reed wearing them.

Unsurprisingly, the teddy bear look never caught on, 1970s.

A cuddly twosome make it hard to choose, 1970.

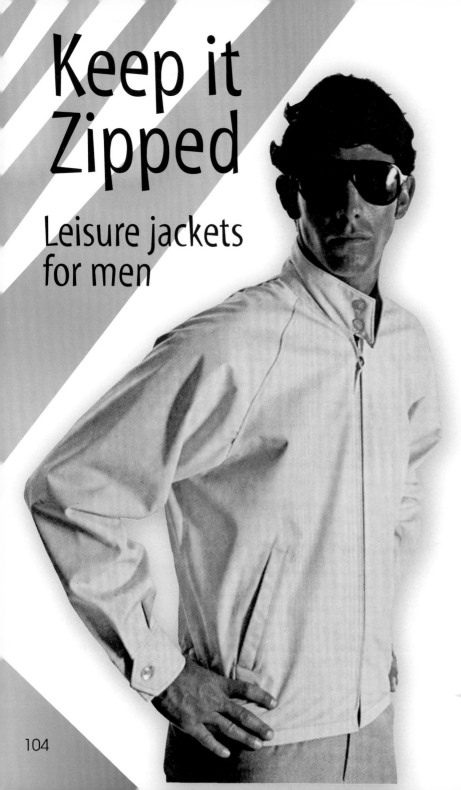

Keep it Zipped

Leisure jackets for men

Any similarity between the 'bum freezer' jackets of the 1970s and the macho leather and MA1 jackets of air force pilots and ton-up rockers is purely coincidental. Men's collarless leisure jackets, whether they were in leather or shiny cotton poplin, especially in pale colours, should have been banished along with synthetic permanent pleat trousers. There have been several variations of this style of man's jacket, some infinitely more popular than others, including the Harrington, favourite of the skinheads and worn together with Ben Sherman button-down shirts, StaPrest trousers or Levi's, and, of course, a shaven head.

Although this style of jacket has been around for a generation or two in the armed forces, the man to blame for bringing it on to the High Street was Pierre Cardin, who created shock waves with his cut-off bomber jackets in woollen tweeds

A man of action in yellow poplin, 1970s.

Looks like leather – but it's chintz – which is worse? 1970s.

Casual style. The flair, the care and of course, the value from Man at C&A. Chintz blousons with cord trim. Choice of colours. Chest 86–107cm (34–42")
£16 99
Easy care polyester trousers. Waist 81–107cm (32–42")
£11 99

A WORLD OF CLOTHES

C&A
Compare our prices, anywhere.

Best-forgotten Fashions
Fake leather coats
they make you crack up

in 1960 – still favoured by George W. Bush today. This just encouraged men to think that they could look good in a blouson style. Why didn't they look good? Because slim as men's hips might be, these jackets cut across the bottom at the worst possible place and the pockets soon filled up with loose change and handkerchiefs and looked like hamsters' cheeks. Along with big hair and big shades, the leisure jacket should have stayed hidden.

Stuffin' and puffin'

Padded jackets

It is strange to think that the infamous gangsta-rap puffa jacket, so beloved of baggy-trousered 'bovver' boys, originated in the 1980s as a genteel gilet which kept country ladies warm while walking the labradors. It became the ultimate Sloane accessory when young Lady Diana Spencer was photographed wearing one. Whether it is filled with duck down or synthetic stuffing, the puffa jacket, and now the puffa coat, does not seem to want to go away. The true Puffa® jacket is made with patented processes, either Puffatex or Puffafill, designed to cope with the vagaries of the weather in the British countryside, and is sold mainly from shops in tents at horse trials across the land, alongside green wellies and Barbour jackets.

Does it come in yellow? Minnie Driver goes for maximum impact, 2000s.

It is all a long way away from the puffa jacket's new incarnation as the chav's jacket of choice. Young, unemployed, but still with the money for the latest sports gear, no self-respecting chavette would be seen on the streets without the latest enormous Fila puffa jacket, tracksuit bottoms, hooped 'gold' earrings and Burberry bag. But beware – this is the jacket that turns even the skinniest body into a Michelin man. Lucky for 5-year-old Mark Rayner it did. In the winter of 1997, he was pushed into a freezing lake and survived only because his puffa jacket kept him afloat.

In the 1980s, only the poshest folks got puffed up, 1988.

8

It'll Never Catch On . . . and it Didn't

Heavy Metal

Metallic clothing

In 1968, Spanish-born Paris-based designer Paco Rabanne grabbed the headlines by creating a mini dress made from lacquered hole-punched aluminium discs. As he said in 1966, 'I defy anyone to design a hat, coat or dress that hasn't been done before. The only new frontier left in fashion is the finding of new materials.' He had started his business in Paris making boleros of multi-coloured cellulose acetate 'Rhodoid' plastic discs. Soon, his Rhodoid earring designs were seen in every stylish magazine. His first official collection called 'Mec'art', which comprised just twelve items, was modelled

French chanteuse Françoise Hardy looked weighed down by her metallic suit, 1968.

by barefoot models to the music of Pierre Boulez's
'Le marteau sans maître'.

   Rabanne prided himself on making 'unwearable
dresses made of contemporary materials'. Coco Chanel's
squashing response was, 'he's not a couturier, he's a
metal worker'. In the late 1960s, French pop singer
Françoise Hardy strolled through London's
Embankment Gardens wearing a metallic all-in-one
suit that had taken her an hour to put on – no wonder,
it weighed 16kg. Not surprising then that metal outfits
did not catch on. For much the same reason that
medieval soldiers gave up wearing chain mail centuries
ago – they are heavy, clanky and uncomfortable and
there are far better alternatives.

A metal mini dress with lacquered
aluminium discs from Wacko Paco's
collection, 1968.

Bin That Dress

Paper clothes

In the 1960s, paper clothes were hailed as the way forward. Today you come across them only in hospitals and at embarrassing waxing sessions at the beauty salon. The 'Paper Caper' was the first disposable dress produced by the US Scott Paper Company in 1966. Part of a promotion for Scott's paper towels, they cost $1 and quickly sold over half a million. But the colour rubbed off if the dress got wet, and worse, the paper 'fabric' was not only not very strong and could tear, but it was also a fire hazard. Soon flame-resistant versions were being produced, including an Andy Warhol version with Campbell's Soup cans printed all over it.

In London, Ossie Clark and Celia Birtwell had fun with paper designs and Miss Selfridge sold paper dresses but

HORRIBLE HATS
Pillbox hats
they looked silly, even on Diana

Sensible yes, but sexy never, 1960s.

customers kept tearing the hems to see if they were really made from paper. A stronger non-woven material using by-products such as wood pulp with a rayon mesh appeared later. Cheap to produce, the 'fabric' could be screen-printed with any photographic image. Predictions by enthusiastic paper products executives that by 1980 one in four items of clothing would be disposable proved disastrously wrong.

Disposable dresses by French designer Daniel Hechter, 1966.

Transparent clothes

The arrival of clear malleable PVC fabric sent 1960s designers into a frenzy of creativity coming up with crazy designs such as Teddy Tinling's tennis dress worn by Wimbledon champion, Brazilian Maria Bueno in 1966. John Bates, the name behind 1960s TV hit show *The Avengers* design label Jean Varon, made see-through mini skirts designed to be worn over swimming costumes. In the US, Betsey Johnson made a clear plastic dress for New York boutique Paraphernalia, which came complete with a set of squiggles to be stuck on in appropriate places.

HORRIBLE HATS
Racoon skin caps
a furry silly hat – thanks,
Davy Crockett

Teddy Tinling gave Brazilian tennis ace Maria Bueno a PVC midriff, 1966.

But there were two clear problems. Clothes are usually supposed to cover up parts of the body. And PVC is notoriously hot and sticky. So what was the point in wearing two layers of clothes when one would do? There is no point to it – which is probably why the only plastic see-through item that has stayed the course is the plastic rain hat as worn by little old ladies on coach outings to Bournemouth.

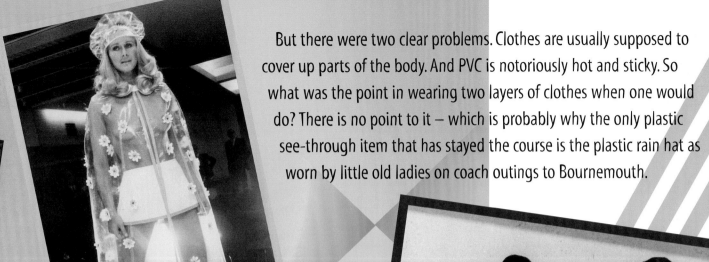

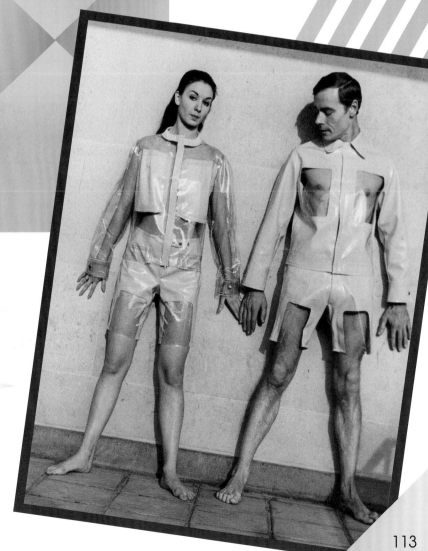

A Berketex flower-scattered clear plastic rain cape reveals all, 1968.

In the 1960s, these scanty PVC sailing suits with windows seemed like a good idea, 1966.

Best-forgotten Fashions
Donkey jackets
best kept on the building site

113

9

And To Go With It

Did Granddad ever wear them?

Round glasses

The essential accessory at late 1960s pop festivals, 1967.

The 1960s and 1970s were definitely the time for silly glasses, the silliest probably being glassless glasses. It all started with John Lennon. If it had not been for him wearing round glasses, they might never have become the fashion accessory of the 1960s. But Lennon did actually need to wear glasses and he really would not have looked right in a pair of Buddy Holly horn-rims. Unbelievably, but true, in 2002, The Beatles Story museum in Liverpool bought the pair of glasses John Lennon wore from 1970 to 1973 for £1 million to display in its collection.

Glasses king used to be Elton John, who owned around 4,000 pairs when he had laser surgery in 2003. He said he was tired of never being able to find them. Sir Elton's outrageous spectacles were part of his image and he admitted to having bought 20,000 pairs over the years, including glasses with windscreen wipers, flashing

HORRIBLE HATS

Bandanas

the Willie Nelson look

lights and sun visors. There was even a West End comedy called *Elton John's Glasses*, in which his beloved football team Watford lost the 1984 FA Cup Final when the goalkeeper was blinded by a flash of sunlight reflected on the star's specs.

One of Elton John's more restrained pairs of glasses, 1978.

A commercial take on the John Lennon look, 1970.

WHAT'S THAT SMELL?

It was money down the drain for *Ab Fab*'s favourite designer, Christian Lacroix, the first new couture house to have opened in Paris in twenty years, when, in 1990, he tried to launch his new perfume, C'est La Vie. Not only was it the opposite of the easy, wearable fragrances popular at that time, but the bottle, designed by trendy interior design partnership Garouste and Bonette, was an anatomical heart shape with aortas as the stopper: it failed to make its mark as 'the pulse of life'.

AND TO CAP IT ALL

Caps for men

In the 1960s, for the first time since the 1930s, young men starting wearing hats again. What could possibly have been the reason? Surely they didn't need one to doff to every passing lady and vicar they met? That sort of street etiquette had disappeared decades before. Hair was long enough to keep your head warm. Yet, unforgivably, young men started wearing rather strange leather caps, making them look like Russian refugee sea captains.

The Mods may have had their little pork pie trilbies, but for the swinging sixties' man the only thing to be seen in was the soft cap, ideally in leather but more often in denim or cotton. An advertisement in a 1964 copy of *Mersey Beat* advertised 'Beatle Caps produced by Kangol … a fashion trend that could catch on … in eleven different colours'. It could have been yet another Pierre Cardin design that Brian Epstein had grabbed for the publicity-conscious boys from Liverpool. More likely, Epstein was tapping into the latest trends from Carnaby Street, which had become the world centre for street fashion in the 1960s.

US rock guitarist Johnny Winter wearing a cool corduroy cap, 1969.

Bonjour matelots – no outfit was complete without a complement of caps, 1967.

HORRIBLE HATS
Baseball caps
any way round

116

The *bigger* the better – or not

Big bow ties

Bow ties have been around since the nineteenth century when they had silly names like the 'Butterfly' and the 'Batswing', and by the 1960s nothing else would do for evening wear in any colour as long as it was black. But then came the colour revolution. Not since the eighteenth century had men worn such a rainbow assortment of colours in suits, shirts and ties. In the words of the song from the 1968 musical *Hair*, this was nothing more than man's emergence 'from his drab

Not just any old prat, but a complete one, 1974.

118

camouflage into the gaudy plumage which is the birthright of his sex'. Flamboyancy ruled and what could be more flamboyant than a bow tie? A bigger bow tie!

Op Art and Pop Art styles looked great with a Bonzo Dog Do-Da band style of dressing but how many men could get away with that? Writer Angus McGill claimed that the bow tie was a 'garment that combines confident flourish with absolute respectability', admitting that once he put his on, he became 'as bumptious as bow-tie wearers everywhere'. The fashion for big bow ties did not last beyond the early 1970s. From then on only the odd eccentric and circus clown is ever seen wearing them.

Take away the bow tie — and it was still an awful outfit, 1970.

HORRIBLE HATS
Berets
'allo, 'allo, what eez that on your 'ead?

119

A Handbag?

Handbags for men

While men always wonder what women carry in their handbags, women often wonder how on earth men manage without one. In the late 1960s, they did not have to. Designers André Bardot, Jose Camps, Socrate, Gaston Waltener and Max Evzeline, known as the Group of Five, showed haute couture menswear in Paris and caused a sensation by including men's handbags – or 'man cases' as they called them – in their collection. With the fashion for trousers to be so tight at that time that there was nowhere to put your packet of Gauloise, 'man cases' seemed the ideal answer. Soon variations were seen in all the smart restaurants and offices as men across Europe

What did men keep in their handbags? The mystery remains, 1960s.

ditched the briefcase for a shoulder-slung handbag.

But just as one was rather suspicious of a man who kept his loose change in a purse, there was something decidedly dodgy about a man with a handbag in the 1970s. What did he keep in there? These were the days before mobile phones and PDAs. A comb, a wallet, and a clean white handkerchief? Too small to carry papers in, too big for just a packet of cigarettes and a lighter. Men soon realised that they had no need for a handbag and, quite rightly, dumped this suspicious accessory.

The handbag was never a completely cool accessory, 1970s.

Something Fishy

Kipper ties

HORRIBLE HAIR
CREW CUTS
all-American cu(l)t

Every man wanted his tie to be bigger than the next man's, 1970s.

For a few years in the late 1960s and early 1970s, ties became as wide as … a kipper, and as colourful as a sea full of tropical fish. Which was appropriate since it was designer Michael Fish who started the craze for wide ties when he opened his shop 'Mr Fish' in 1966 in London's Clifford Street, just off the famous tailors' road, Savile Row. Having graduated from working in top menswear supplier Turnbull & Asser in super-smart Jermyn Street, Michael Fish soon had rock stars and celebrities clamouring for his styles.

But, in truth, it was the Duke of Windsor who first started the vogue for kipper ties in the 1930s. Most people thought he got the fatter knot style from an extra twist of the tie. In fact, he just ordered his ties wider and lined with thicker silk – so for kipper, substitute Windsor. Unfortunately, the Duke of Windsor's and Michael Fish's imitators were not so stylish. In the 1970s, no man's wardrobe was complete without a handful of horrors such as those proudly shown off by star footballer Alan Hudson. Bigger ties meant bigger knots as well, a style that did not suit many men, even if they did know how to tie the 'big-knot four-in-hand', still known as the Windsor knot.

Footballer Alan Hudson had dozens of kipper ties in his wardrobe, 1970.

HORRIBLE HAIR

DA
dead awful

FLYING FRINGES

Worst pop group hairstyle award goes to A Flock of Seagulls. A 'New Wave' band formed in 1980 by Liverpudlian ex-hairdresser Mike Score and his brother, Ali, the group were best known for their ridiculous hairstyles orchestrated by Mike. Few people remember their US hit 'I Ran', but plenty can visualise the long cow's lick flicked up fringes – and wish they couldn't. Even Duran Duran's John Taylor's quiff wasn't quite as silly as these.

Keeping legs warm

Legwarmers

Any girl who saw the dance hit of the 1980s, *Fame*, rushed out and bought a pair of legwarmers in some hideous fluorescent colour just so she could be like the stars of the New York City High School of Performing Arts. She had probably never been near a dance studio and would not know her Pineapple from a pineapple. This did not stop legwarmers from becoming the must-have accessory of the era, leading to legs looking like *Last of the Summer Wine* Nora Batty's saggy stockings. There have been dangerous moments recently when it seemed as though the passion for legwarmers might be revived (has it ever gone among the cult fashion group, the 'Fruits' in Japan?), but they only seem to be seen, oddly enough, among the punks of Camden Town.

Legwarmers are not alone among the silly leg fashions. Sock shoes – shoes with knee-length socks attached – not surprisingly did not catch on. Striped tube socks did, unfortunately, despite the fact that everyone should have known that circular stripes are never flattering. Then there were toe socks. Although there were claims that toe socks helped avoid bunions and corns, in the 1970s they were just plain fun, brightly coloured and with yet more stripes. They are surely the only accessory to have a dedicated fan website (http://fan.spiffy-ness.ca/toesocks) devoted to them with fans from Pakistan to Peru, and from Andorra to Australia.

HORRIBLE HAIR
CRIMPED HAIR
flat and frizzy

Wrinkly legs were all the rage, 1982.

Red-legged but not red-faced in 1980s legwarmers.

What a bummer!

Bum bags

Sometimes an idea comes along that on paper looks really good. Why not strap your bag round your waist instead of slinging it over your shoulder where it's vulnerable to being snatched? That way you would know immediately if anyone was trying to get their hands on your valuables. If this made sense on the ski slope then why not on the way to the shops or the gym? So, in the 1980s, bum bags (or fanny packs as they were known in the States) became the perfect accompaniment to the track or shell suit,

Jonathan King looked suitably embarrassed to be wearing his bum bag back to front, 1998.

leggings or cycle shorts outfit, just the size for keys, money and not much else given the size of mobile cell phones back then.

The only trouble was that first, wearing your bum bag at the back really did make your bum look big and second, it was still an open invitation for someone to slip their hand into your belongings. So bum bags became tum bags and a low-slung tum at that. Nowadays the only excuse to wear one is when you are running a stall at a car boot or jumble sale.

HORRIBLE HAIR
SIDEBURNS
no excuses

Actress Mary Crosby looking ready to help out at a local jumble sale, 2003.

Hair Raisers

A little dab'll do you

Brylcreem

Brylcreem, a little dab'll do you!
Brylcreem, you look so debonair!
The gals will all pursue ya,
They'll love to get their fingers in your hair. . .

Brylcreem was the first men's hair product to be mass marketed and by the 1950s no self-respecting star of stage or screen was without his 'little dab' to keep his hair in place. Not many 'gals' enjoyed running their fingers through the mixture of mineral oil, beeswax, fragrance and chemicals, but it remained the top-selling hair product for men, promoted by the Brylcreem boy himself, England cricketer Dennis Compton.

LET YOUR SCALP BREATHE... ENCOURAGE YOUR HAIR TO LIVE

BRYLCREEM
grooms by surface tension

for smart, healthy hair

In the 1950s, Brylcreem was in every man's bathroom, 1954.

Little wonder sales of Brylcreem plummeted, 1970s.

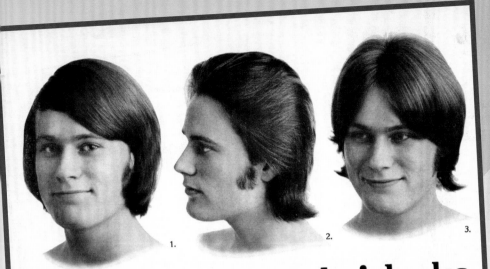

change the way your hair looks.
Without cutting it.

Side hair is groomed under and towards your cheek. Top hair goes to the side, then back away from your face.

If your hair has a mind of its own, use a spray of Brylcreem Soft Hair Dry Spray with Protein before you start blow-drying. It does two important things for longer hair: conditions and controls. Spray it on, then massage it into your hair and scalp. The protein penetrates your hair shafts, helping to protect your hair from the parching effect of blow-drying. And the styling control of Soft Hair will help you get your hair going where you want it. And keep it there.

2. No part

If you can't be bothered with blow-drying or you'd like to look more mature, try this.

Spray your towel-dried hair with Soft Hair Dry Spray with Protein and massage it in. This puts styling control where you need it: down deep in your hair.

Then, with your brush, groom all your hair straight back against your head. You've got a forehead again. Earlobes, too. Flip the hair at your neck out and up.

Use the brush at the crown to lift your hair and turn it under. This gives a little extra height where you may need it.

Another spritz of Soft Hair where your natural part may be trying to appear will help prevent it from doing so.

3. Center part

The last time you parted your hair on the side it either fell in your food or made you look lopsided. Try a center part instead.

With your hot-comb or blow-dryer, turn your hair forward and under on either side of the part. Starting from the part, your hair should go away from your forehead, towards your cheek and back to your ear. An S-shape. This makes your hair flip out at the bottom.

From the end of the part down the back of your head, all hair goes up and under, for fullness. At the very bottom make the ends flip by turning them up.

And don't forget Soft Hair Dry Spray with Protein. Its conditioners will counteract the drying effects of a hot-comb or blow-dryer. And it'll control your hair while keeping it healthy-looking.

After all, if your hair is dull and dried out, all the styling in the world won't help the way you look. That's why, no matter what style you decide on, we've got a product that will help you.

The Brylcreem® group.

We've come a long way since "a little dab will do ya."

Then in the early 1960s, along came four lads from Liverpool with their swinging fringes. Kept going by middle-aged men and 'greasers' who used it to create their DA hairstyles, Brylcreem's days seemed numbered. Even John Travolta, as 'Danny Zuko' in the aptly named 1978 smash hit *Grease*, with his slicked-back style, failed to return Brylcreem's profits to their heady heights of the 1950s. Salvation was at hand: the 'new man' of the 1990s discovered hair 'products'. David Beckham signed with Brylcreem for a reported £4m in the 1990s. Gels and sprays began appearing in the bathroom and demand for the ultimate 'pomade' was back. As they say in the Brylcreem ad of today, 'the right stuff for today's hairstyles is the same as it was in 1929'. But do 'gals' want to run their fingers through hair coated with oil and wax? No more than they did in 1929.

Back Comb in the UK

Beehive hairstyles

Pop princess Helen Shapiro sported a classic beehive hairdo, 1960s.

Worst Women's Hairstyle

In the late 1950s and early 1960s, before the days of synthetic wigs and hairpieces, creating the latest style was hard work – hard on the arms and hard on the hair. Ages was spent holding up little clumps of hair and then furiously backcombing until they could stand up on their own – killing the biceps and ruining the hair. The hairspray used, often Aqua Net for its shellac-like qualities, formed a helmet over the hair, invisible to all but only too apparent to touch. Even worse was trying to get rid of the spray and twisted knots at the end of the day without losing clumps of hair. No wonder many didn't bother and just went once a week to the local salon for a 'comb-out'.

Queen of the beehive was 1960s star Dusty Springfield, closely followed by teenage singing sensation Helen Shapiro. Where will you find the beehive now? Only on ladies of a certain age with time and money to spend at the hairdressers – women such as Lady Thatcher, who since her makeover in the 1970s has turned to

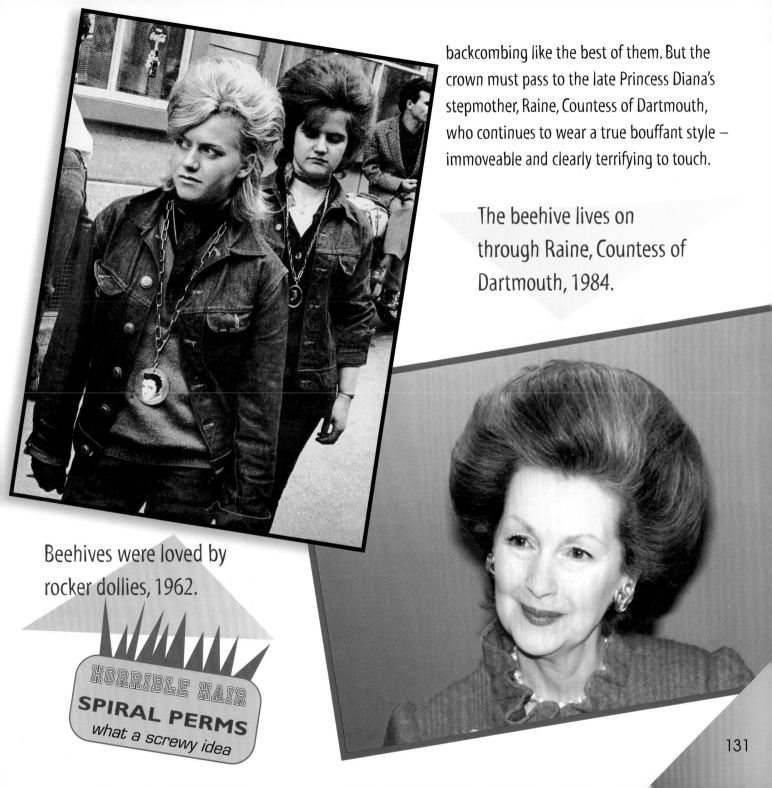

backcombing like the best of them. But the crown must pass to the late Princess Diana's stepmother, Raine, Countess of Dartmouth, who continues to wear a true bouffant style – immoveable and clearly terrifying to touch.

The beehive lives on through Raine, Countess of Dartmouth, 1984.

Beehives were loved by rocker dollies, 1962.

HORRIBLE HAIR
SPIRAL PERMS
what a screwy idea

Black Hair Day

Afro hairstyles

The Afro, one of the most instantly recognisable hairstyles of the late 1960s and early 1970s, grew out of the rise of black pride and the civil rights movement in the US. With young white boys ditching their crew cuts first for a Beatles look and then the long-haired hippie style, black militants were left looking decidedly conservative with their close crop cuts. Even early pictures of activist Malcolm X show him with a slicked-back straightening style. Then after years of struggling with Teda and Magic Hair Straightening kits, or in the US, the Yvette Home Hair Straightening Kit, suddenly it was hip to have the frizz – and the bigger the better.

The style quickly spread from anti-establishment figures such as Angela Davis into the pop and film world. All five of the Jacksons were keen early-Afro wearers as were Diana Ross and Marsha Hunt and a host of black groups like The Chi-Lites and The Chairman of the Board. But this was no low-maintenance look. Special five-pronged combs were needed to get that bushiness and were constantly being whipped out to give the style a fluff-up. White guys and girls who didn't want to be left

White afros were not on the whole successful, 1967.

HORRIBLE HAIR
DREADLOCKS
pass the scissors

132

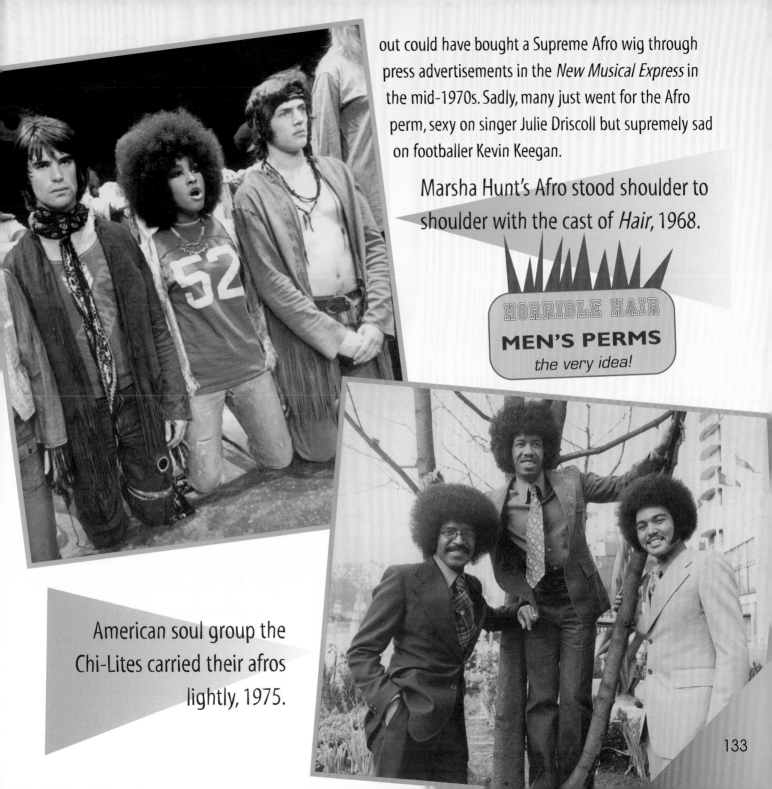

out could have bought a Supreme Afro wig through press advertisements in the *New Musical Express* in the mid-1970s. Sadly, many just went for the Afro perm, sexy on singer Julie Driscoll but supremely sad on footballer Kevin Keegan.

Marsha Hunt's Afro stood shoulder to shoulder with the cast of *Hair*, 1968.

HORRIBLE HAIR

MEN'S PERMS
the very idea!

American soul group the Chi-Lites carried their afros lightly, 1975.

A Right Wigging

Synthetic wigs

Just as artificial fabrics were all the rage in the 1960s, synthetic fibres such as Dynel were claimed as the answer to all those bad hair days. Who needed to go to Vidal Sassoon when you could buy the perfect hairstyle off the shelf in twenty different colours? No department store was without its wig and hairpiece stand, and no girl's wardrobe was without a selection of short and long styles. In 1970, it was estimated that one in three women owned a wig.

Advertisements claimed that synthetic hair was far easier to maintain than human hair. Most synthetic styles were pre-set, which was a keen selling point – 'one never has to waste time with arduous styling sessions'. The payback was that these wigs looked about as natural as a My Little Pony's tail and as full of

Do you really know a good wig when you see one?

How to style it easily and quickly?

Which type naturally matches your face and colouring?

A hairdresser knows. That's why GinchyWigs are sold only by hairdressers. They can tell you how to put a GinchyWig on. How to flick it into style. How to keep it beautifully in shape.

You'd look great in a GinchyWig.

Ask your hairdresser to show you.

Illustrated: GinchyWig 86.

GinchyWig

The wig a hairdresser knows is best

'Easily styled' synthetic wigs took the care out of hair, 1960s.

static as Barbie or Sindy's hair after a good brushing. And it meant carrying a bagful of Kirbigrips, in case the thing started slipping, and just hoping that that hot date wasn't going to want to run his fingers through your hair as the evening wore on.

False hair flourished again briefly in the early 1980s when Bo Derek's beaded cornrows from the movie *10*

became a funky fashion moment and produced a flurry of fakes which now only surface at fancy dress parties. Final nail in the coffin: in 2005, find-it directory Yellow Pages announced it was dropping the hairpiece manufacturers' categories.

Build a Wig Wardrobe

A different look for each day of the week, 1970s.

HORRIBLE HAIR
SIDE PONYTAILS
Britney, please!

What's That on your Lip?

Droopy moustaches

Whatever you call it – a walrus, a horse-shoe, a chevron, a painter's brush or, most famously, a Zapata – the droopy moustache has no place on a man's face. Perhaps if you've got the brains of Lloyd George – or even better, Albert Einstein – then you can be excused, but anyone else under fifty sporting this 'hairy mouth awning' should have realised that they were on very dangerous ground. You just have to look at the track record of the Zapata. Who remembers the crimes Tom Selleck's Magnum PI solved on Hawaii when you couldn't take your eyes off his 'tache?

The world of sport produced a few howlers as

MOHICAN
even David Beckham looked silly

well. Stand up racing ace, Nigel Mansell, decathlete Daley Thompson, and cricketer Ian Botham, known as 'Beefy' to his friends – no doubt for what they could see on his top lip after lunch. Could their role model possibly have been that King of the Moustache, actor Peter Wyngarde? No hiding behind his TV persona, Jason King, Wyngarde went on wearing his fringed lip for years. Nowadays, time-warp-trapped sports commentator Des Lynam keeps the furry flag flying, but surely Sacha Baron-Cohen's Borat is closer to being today's moustache master.

The most famous moustache of the decade, 1970s.

No hint of irony on this 1970s model's face, 1970.

Comb Up and See Me

Big hair for men

Come the 1970s, for the first time for decades, men were putting something other than Brylcreem on their hair. The Beatles cut was dead, and the long-haired hippy look long gone. New words crept into barbers' vocabularies, words such as 'style', 'blow dry' and 'products' – and this was not just for the weekend. Big hair for men meant time in front of the mirror, comb in hand.

This could all have been a bit sissy if male role models such as England and West Ham football star Geoff Hurst weren't seen about town with a handsome head of big hair the envy of his mates. Advertisements for the new Remington Hot Comb for Men showed before and after pictures of Manchester City footballer Rodney

HORRIBLE HAIR
SHAVED HEAD
à la Sinéad O'Connor

A pride of Osmonds set hairstyling standards, 1970s.

Marsh, rough and ready kicking the ball, but smooth and big haired out of the changing room. By the 1990s, the only people to have big hair were middle-class suburban housewives still tied to the weekly visit to the hairdresser – and perma-tan TV presenter David Dickinson, topping a 2004 poll of worst celebrity hairstyles. Nowadays, pop stars and footballers are more likely to get their big hair by extensions, false strands glued on to their own hair, for instant length and lustre.

Big ties, big collars, big flares – and, of course, big hair to match, 1970s.

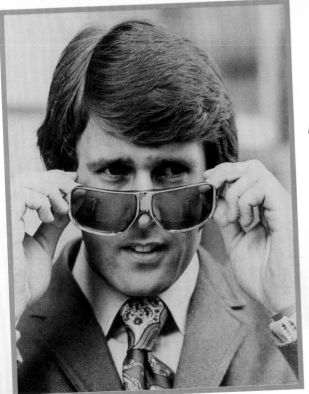

Not a hair out of place for England footballer, Geoff Hurst, 1971.

139

Marvel at the Mullet

The mullet

In 2004, David Beckham's mohican hair cut was voted the most memorable haircut in sport, knocking Sir Bobbie Charlton's comb-over into second, and ex-England goalkeeper David Seaman's pony tail into seventh. What about the mullet, we hear you scream. Short on top, long at the back, the mullet has been around a long time – just look at Oliver Cromwell – but the 1970s and 1980s saw its popularity peak.

There is only one hairstyle for men that has books and websites devoted to it and that is the most infamous men's haircut in sport or anywhere. Indeed, more places were taken

The long and the short of footballer Mark Wright's mullet style, 1980s.

in this hairy top-twenty list by mullets than any other style. Stand up André Agassi, Andy Fordham and Ian Botham. They were guilty of one of the greatest crimes against hair ever perpetrated. It is a crime also committed by a long list of other miscreants from singer Michael Bolton to aged nightclub owner Peter Stringfellow. But even top stars like Mel Gibson in *Lethal Weapon*, Jean-Claude Van Damme in *Hard Target* and Adam Sandler in *The Wedding Singer* have been guilty of getting in touch with their feminine side with this shoulder-sweeping hairstyle – not to mention Britain's own Prime Minister, Tony Blair.

Will Tony Blair ever apologise for his misjudged mullet? 1987.

Eat Your Heart Out, Miss Piggy

Big hair for women

As anyone who has got through half a can of hairspray in one evening knows, big hair is not the same as a beehive. Along with big ties and big shoulders – and that's just the women – the big hair of the 1970s said far more about who you thought you were than the beehive ever did. It said, 'I'm a strong woman but I'm pretty and feminine as well'. It also said, 'Don't touch my hair – I've worked hard to get it looking this good!'

The most famous Queen of the Big Hair dynasty was Charlie's Angel Farrah Fawcett. Her sun-lit locks became the envy of every girl whose arms ached from hours of standing in front of a mirror holding on to her curling tongs trying to achieve the

Queen of big hair, Farrah Fawcett with her crowning glory, 1978.

same effect. Enormous rollers with Velcro-like hooks were produced to help give 'body'. Women retreated under drying hoods again for the first time since the 1950s. Hair had to look natural and swing as one walked so that, just like in the TV advertisement, men in the street would ask, 'Is she? Isn't she?' wearing hairspray. She was, of course – if there was any left after the men in the house had hit the bathroom.

US star Loni Anderson showing off the look so many aspired to, 1979.

11

These Shoes Weren't Made for Walking

Pick your way out of this one

Winkle-pickers

According to Marilyn Monroe, stiletto heels were the most flattering thing to happen to legs. In contrast, winkle-pickers in the early 1960s did few favours for either the women or men who wore them. Girls had to buy shoes two sizes too big to get their feet in. Rumour has it that some even resorted to having their little toes surgically removed to get into these slim pointy monstrosities,

Pointed street style in the early 1960s.

144

The longer the better for ace '**winkle-pickers**', 1960.

prompting one foot doctor to exclaim: 'Teenagers ... are becoming addicted to court shoes, pencil-heeled with toes as sharp as the fangs of the biblical serpent.'

Boys squirmed their feet into hideous concoctions: 'Grey pearlized imitation crocodile, plastic sole, 1½in stacked heel and winkle-picker toe – styled in Italy', cooed one advertisement. Although they might have been inspired by the styles of the young blacks and Hispanics of Harlem, and whether they were called 'pointed Spanish toes', 'needle toes', or 'modern tapered toe, Italian inspired', winkle-pickers were as British as the drainpipe trousers with which they were worn, and just as unflattering. It only needed the toe to curl up at the end for them to look like a pair of medieval poulaine shoes. By the mid-1960s, their days were numbered as wider trousers led to another fashion disaster – platforms.

What's up, Doc? Dr Martens

ALSO RANS
Metal taps
strictly for the
soldiers

Instantly recognisable from its look and its name, even its initials – DMs – are enough to conjure up images of 'bovver boys' and football hooligans. The revolutionary air-cushioned sole was first thought of by a young German, Klaus Maertens, who began producing comfortable shoes for the older woman. This was a big stride towards becoming the must-have footwear for every skinhead in Britain and then a fashion item in its own right worn by pop stars and top models alike. Skinheads made them

part of their street 'uniform' in the 1970s, and football hooligans took to wearing DMs when more lethal footwear with steel caps and spikes was banned from grounds. When pop groups such as The Who and the Bay City Rollers slammed on stage with their cherry-red 1460s (named after the date of their launch in the UK, 1 April 1960) every teenager wanted a pair.

But then the trainer arrived and Doc Martens disappeared from the playground and the club scene. Even the sight of Kate Winslet complete with DMs, miles of leg and mini skirt could not save the company from near collapse. Only a handful of Goths, punks and postmen remained loyal. Sales crashed from £235m in 1999 to £90m in 2003. Profits nose-dived and the company made a loss of £62m in 2003. Will Dr Martens ever reclaim their place as sub-cultural icons? Every Doc has its day, and it seems as if this medical masterpiece has had its.

In the 1970s, DMs were the only boot to be seen in, 1974.

Kate Winslet putting in the boot at Heathrow, 1998.

ALSO RANS
Brothel creepers
how low can you get?

Step this way for a mighty fall

Platform shoes for women

In the early 1970s, no outfit was complete without white platforms, 1971.

Who is to blame for inventing the platform shoe, that arch ankle-sprainer that rode so high in the 1970s? Famous shoemakers Roger Vivier and Salvatore Ferragamo can each lay claim to this dubious title since they were both making startlingly high platforms way back in the 1930s. Vivier said he drew his inspiration for his early designs from orthopaedic shoes and no one would disagree with him there.

Amazingly, Paloma Picasso actually wanted to take responsibility for the new arrival of platforms in the late 1960s. But it was Biba which sold 75,000

Naomi Campbell seeing the joke of Vivienne Westwood's horrors, 1993.

Baby Spice Emma Bunton and one of her pairs of ankle-breaking trainers, 1997.

of its 5in heeled platform suede boots in 1968. By the 1970s, Terry de Havilland was infamous for his hideous creations, each one a mixture of coloured snakeskin. No surprise that he says he thought up most of his wild designs while on acid trips. What did he have printed on his business card? 'Cobblers to the world'! Sentiments surely seconded by Vivienne Westwood when she sent Naomi Campbell tottering down the catwalk in her 6in platforms in 1993. Even in the 1990s, Baby Spice Emma Bunton strutted her stuff in a pair of 6in platform Buffalo trainers. This is a grotesque fashion that never dies. In 1999, the British

Standards Institute wanted to introduce a kite mark to protect people from their footwear after a Japanese student fell off her shoes and fractured her skull. Will they never learn? Platforms are the pits.

ALSO RANS
Converse All-Star
canvas comfort
with a high top

149

The Height of Bad Taste

Platform shoes for men

If women looked ridiculous in platforms, then men looked even worse. The 1970s was the zenith of foul footwear. As trousers got wider and wider, shoes got higher and higher. Giving the Chelsea boot the boot in the early 1970s, few men minded the extra height platforms gave them, especially not Gary Glitter in his 3in silver stompers. No self-respecting pop star was without his closet full of high-heeled hoppers. Isaac Hayes, writer of the great 'Shaft' theme for the ultimate 'blaxploitation' movie of the 1970s, owned twenty-seven pairs of skin-tight, thigh-high platform boots.

But king of clompers was Elton John who used Los Angeles designer Mundo to make some of his most outrageous hand-painted platform boots. Beaded, monogrammed, glitzy and ghastly, John's platform boots were deliciously outrageous on stage, but prompted idiotic imitations on the high street.

Nothing quite beat Harold Smerling's 'goldfish' platforms, which hit the headlines in 1972.

ALSO RANS
Chelsea boots
pull-on pointies

1970s high street show of footwear fashions for men, 1973.

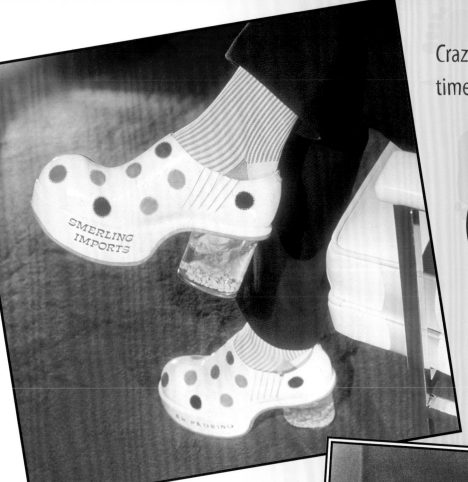
SMERLING IMPORTS

EL PADRINO

Crazy shoes for the crazy fashion times of the early 1970s.

Clumpy Carnaby Street clompers for the sure-footed, 1975.

Thank goodness, by the end of the 1970s, shoes were coming down to earth again and, like John Travolta's *Saturday Night Fever* platforms, relegated to the back of the wardrobe, to be brought out and peeked at once in a while as 'Exhibit A' of hideous footwear.

151

Batty Boots

Odd boots

Before the 1960s, boots were something you wore for riding or taking the dog for a walk across a muddy field. Then in 1964 Paris-based designer Courrèges changed everything with his space-age collection including flat white boots with cut-outs at the top. Soon, white boots were the must-have footwear accessory included in every new fashion collection. This was helped by the introduction of Corfam, a Du Pont product, that claimed to be 'so great, it's almost better than leather'. Who were they trying to kid?

Lace-up boots completed the mini and hot pant look, 1970.

KING OF THE CLODS

Sir Elton John may have a mantelpiece full of awards already, but even he couldn't deny that at his peak he was also 'king of the clodhoppers'. He still never seems to learn that enough is enough. Four times, Sir Elton has cleared out his closet to raise money for his Aids Foundation charity, piling high loud suits, baseball caps and racks and racks of shoes and boots. Scrutinising a pair of yellow python-skin shoes in 2000, even he groaned and commented, 'There are a few things here that make me think, "Did I really wear that?"' You did, Sir Elton, you did.

ALSO RANS
LA Gear
the 'Moonwalker' special

It didn't look like leather, it didn't stretch to your foot like leather, it didn't breathe like leather, and it squeaked when you walked. But it was just what was needed for the calf-hugging PVC-look boots that flooded the King's Road, spurred on by designs from Mary Quant.

Boots went to new heights in the early 1970s when the craze for platforms went thigh-length as well – just perfect for the cavalier look with hot pants. By the time skirt lengths tumbled, boots were an indispensable part of every girl's wardrobe. Never mind that in white or red vinyl, they made your feet hot and sticky and were hard to get on and off.

Courrèges kept white boots going well into the late 1970s, 1977.

A young Marie Helvin (right) shows off crazy street favourite platforms, 1971.

ALSO RANS
Hush Puppies
a soft option for the 1970s

153

12

Red light District – Go No Further

His 'n' hers

Unisex fashions

Avoid AT ALL COSTS **Anything** *. . . with sequins – strictly not for dancing*

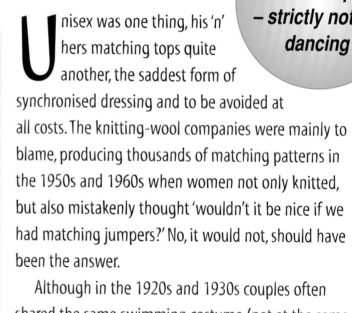

Unisex was one thing, his 'n' hers matching tops quite another, the saddest form of synchronised dressing and to be avoided at all costs. The knitting-wool companies were mainly to blame, producing thousands of matching patterns in the 1950s and 1960s when women not only knitted, but also mistakenly thought 'wouldn't it be nice if we had matching jumpers?' No, it would not, should have been the answer.

Although in the 1920s and 1930s couples often shared the same swimming costume (not at the same time – though they got so baggy when wet, they probably could have done), unisex proper – or 'inter-sex

Acrylic yarns spawned no-no knits such as these, 1970.

clothing' as it was called by the trade – was not born until the late 1960s when it grew out of the hippie look. With both boys and girls wearing long hair, Afghan coats and jeans, it was often hard to tell who was who, or what, from behind. Clothes such as kaftans, granddad shirts and denims were worn by all. But deliberately matching outfits were a definite no-no, be it jumpers, sweatshirts, even anoraks. Only ever excusable on the way to and from a football match, but never cycling or at the gym.

Definitely a couple to be avoided at all costs, 1971.

Personalised sweatshirts were the nadir of his 'n' hers fashion, 1980.

Be the very first with **His & Hers** personalised CREWNECK SWEATSHIRTS **Individually Embroidered** ·NOT PRINTED· WITH YOUR FIRST NAME OR INITIALS ·AT NO EXTRA COST· (Makes an ideal gift) CHOOSE FROM NAVY, SKY BLUE OR BLACK SIZES S. M. L. XL.

JEAN STREET WAREHOUSE 783 STOCKPORT ROAD MANCHESTER 19 REG. IN ENGLAND No. 1747677

No Risk MONEY REFUNDED IF NOT DELIGHTED PROVIDED THE GOODS ARE RETURNED UNUSED WITHIN 14 DAYS OF ARRIVAL

FOR ONLY **£6·99** + 50p p&p per garment

155

Anything Paisley

Paisley

There are some designs that have been round for such a long time that they have just become accepted as good taste. Take chintz: because the designs we see today are based on beautiful eighteenth-century silks, they must be okay. So although one Swedish furniture superstore was rashly exhorting us to 'chuck them out', next season they were selling them again. But there is a place for everything and the place for chintz is in your living-room not on your back. Similarly, just because paisley patterns have been around since Victorian times does not mean they are acceptable as a pattern for men's trousers. Shawls and throws inspired by the Kashmir styles made in this Scottish town are fine, but not as a suiting fabric.

Yet in the 1960s, the paisley pattern was everywhere. Hippies loved its ethnic

King of cool Peter Wyngarde in his paisley coat jacket, 1970s.

Avoid
AT ALL COSTS
Anything
. . . with large logos – so yesterday

156

And the bridegroom wore ... paisley trousers, 1971.

connections and mainstream fabric manufacturers delighted in producing paisley materials in ever more lurid colours. Paisley was printed on to men's velveteen trousers, looking a far cry from the Indian Mughal art that inspired it. And there was no greater swirling dervish than Peter Wyngarde in a paisley coat jacket. But it was once the synthetic fabric manufacturers got hold of it in the 1970s that paisley's days as a fashion fabric were well and truly numbered.

This paisley jacket is more suited to the bathroom than the beach, 1970s.

Scotland Depraved

Bay City Roller Derek Longmuir showed off the band's signature style, 1976.

Tartan

It took Edinburgh's Bay City Rollers four years to have a hit, but when fame arrived in 1971 so did 'The Tartan Army', teenybopper fans who showed their loyalty by wearing tartan just like their idols. But this was no kilted army. Manager Tam Paton thought up the tartan scarf and trouser theme which has done untold harm to the image of the plaid patterns throughout the world. In addition, there were tartan waistcoats, plaid shirts, trimmed ties and just about any item of clothing. But they weren't the first or the last to use Scotland's finest this way. Billy Haley may have shocked UK audiences on his 1957 tour with his rock 'n' roll antics, but it was his backing group, the Comets, who outraged fashion purists by playing in tartan tuxedos.

Another tartan lover who shamelessly sports his country's cloth is Rod Stewart, one of the kings of outrageous rock outfits. The only member of his family to be born in London rather than their native Edinburgh, Stewart at least has a claim to wear one of the hundred genuine clan tartans. Later in the 1980s, punks added tartan to their wardrobes of leather, chains, studs and Mohawk hairstyles – creating just about the strangest interpretation of Scottish clanhood ever seen.

Bay City Rollerettes touting the mix 'n' match tartan look, 1975.

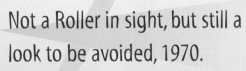

Not a Roller in sight, but still a
look to be avoided, 1970.

Anything fringed

Fringing

Home, home on the range . . . is definitely where anything with fringing should be. It may have looked good on a cowboy, but it is seriously naff on Clapham Common. In the 1950s, Western heroes wore trousers with creases and bootlace ties, and the 'Red Indians' all had beaded headbands and chamois leather leggings. In England in the 1950s, Gerald Manleigh in Oxford Street was offering a 'Buckeroo' shirt: 'the most magnificent authentic Western shirt that money can buy, faultlessly tailored in luxury-textured two-tone Spun Rayon with silk tassels back and front', a snip at 35s 6d.

When movie fashions became more gritty and realistic, and chaps wore chaps and denim jeans, the fringed shirt brigade turned either to Country and Western music or to Native American Indians for style inspiration. Sonny Bono should have known better. Cher at least has some Native American blood credentials, but Sonny was the son of Sicilian immigrants and the Wild West look really doesn't go with the

'Home on the range' – OK for Kansas but not the King's Road, 1970.

The Native American look for Sonny and Cher, 1966.

The Native American look for Sonny and Cher, 1966.

Hippy fringing was easy to come by through mail order, 1960s.

EXCLUSIVE

TOLEDO
Satin-Look. Balloon sleeved, 8" spearpoint, 2" cross-over. Lace-up front. 18" side body zip to ensure true body taper. 6 shades. Black, White, Green, Gold, Royal, Violet.

State neck, chest & waist sizes.

89/6
P/P 2/6

SUEDE FRINGED WAISTLINER
The latest from our sensational Colin Wild original collection. Colours: Gold, Silver Sand, Green, Brown.

£9.9.0
P/P 4/6

pudding basin haircut. Bono's only excuse is that he grew up in California, home to a hundred plywood cowboy film sets. Fringing fitted in with the dress-down hippy culture coming from the West Coast. Yet add a paisley neckerchief and some glittery studs and you were in danger of becoming a 'Rhinestone Cowboy'.

The Press Gang Permanent pressing

In a perfect world, seams would stay straight and pleats would stay pressed. And that's just what manufacturers pledged in the 1950s and 1960s. Throw away that iron! Who is going to need an ironing board any more? Shirts will drip-dry and trousers will always have that 'just pressed' look. This was the future of clothing as promised by textile manufacturers such as Du Pont in the US and Courtaulds in the UK.

The arrival of synthetic fabrics made from petrochemical by-products such as Terylene (known as Dacron in the US) meant that even men's suits could be 'wash-and-wear'. Ladies' skirts with permanent pleats could be thrown in the washing machine and hung up to dry looking as good as new. Not only did the pleats never come out, but also some fabrics even claimed to have a built-in 'soil release – so stains wash out, spots blot off'. So why isn't

Avoid AT ALL COSTS **Anything** . . . *nylon – cling-cling not bling-bling*

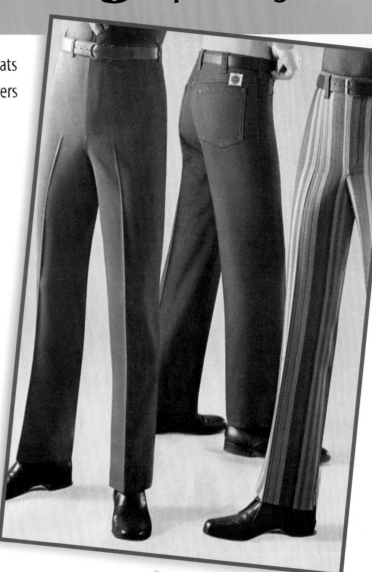

Stitched seams have always been a no-no, 1970.

everyone wearing these new 'wonder' clothes? Because just as Alec Guinness found out in *The Man in the White Suit* (1951) when his suit made of a miracle cloth disintegrated, wonder clothes are rarely as wonderful as they first appear. The advantages of permanent pleats are always offset by their synthetic look and feel.

Don't throw away the iron for these monstrosities, 1970.

Permanently pleated pink nightmare, 1970.

ANYTHING TIE-DYE

Joe Cocker at Woodstock: tied and dyed 'with a little help from my friends', 1969.

Tie-dye

An essential part of the hippy look, tie-dyeing came out of Haight-Ashbury, a San Francisco suburb, in the late 1960s, along with the beads, sandals and everything that rejected the space-age consumerism of artificial fabrics. This look was a long, long way away from the gorgeous designs created by Nigerian women for their national dress, or the Japanese for exotic and intricate kimono and yukata designs. In the UK and the US it was far more hit and miss, with buckets of dye, elastic bands and not forgetting the salt.

Dye companies such as Dylon in the UK and Rit Dye in the States boomed with helpful hints on how to create patterns such as 'dip and rosettes', '2-way strips' and effects such as 'marbled', 'dip dye', 'twists' and 'spirals'.

What could be better than tying knots in a white T-shirt and then dipping it in different dyes so that it came out looking like all the colours of the rainbow? Or waxing out shapes without the skills of the Balinese batikers? Well, pretty well anything unless you really relished looking like a primary school

Avoid AT ALL COSTS **Anything** . . . fake – everyone knows, you know

Sizzler

TIE DYE VESTS
SUPER QUALITY
multi-shaded
T Vests. They're
all the rage and
we've got the
best quality
and colours
Short and Long
Sleeves. State
basic colour
required. Dyed
and delivered to
you by return.
SHORT
SLEEVE **25/-**
p/p 2/6
LONG
SLEEVE **27/6**
p/p 2/6

**CARNABY
FLARES**
Cool
summerweight
'TREVIRA'. As
supplied to many
famous groups.
The snuggest,
closest
fitting waist
seat and top leg
you've ever
worn down to
true flared
bottoms
(20"-26").
Every pair
custom built to
your require-
ments so state
waist, seat, top
leg, inside leg
when ordering.
and bottoms
Latest shades: Yellow, Navy, Red,
Black.
99/6 p/p 4/6

Send S.A.E. for 1970 Leaflet. Group
and Trade enquiries welcome

Dpt. (DYBII)
6 Ganton Street
(off Carnaby Street)
London W1A 4QG

Carnaby Cavern
Personal callers welcome

Tied and dyed just for you from Carnaby Street, 1960s.

project. But plenty did. Put together with the obligatory jeans and long hair and you could go to a rock festival and blend in instantly. You could even have been a rock star, since the likes of Janis Joplin, Joe Cocker and Jimmy Hendrix frequently teamed tie-dye with velvet pants to create the ultimate hip-rock style.

Psychedelic tie-dye lived on at music festivals for years, 1999.

165

Starting to flag

Union Jack

Every few years someone comes up with the not-so-bright idea that making clothes out of the red, white and blue stripes of the Union Jack will be a hot seller. In 1968, Carnaby Street boutiques were selling shirts as part of the 'I'm Backing Britain' campaign. In 1981, bubbly pop group Buck's Fizz won the Eurovision Song Contest with 'Making Your Mind Up', but everyone else's mind was made up that anything with the British national flag on should be sent flying. Even Roger Daltry of *über* pop group The Who quickly rejected this Brit-style in favour of almost as dodgy fringed chamois suede shirts.

Bucks Fizz celebrating their 1980s Eurovision win in patriotic style, 1981.

The most famous Union Jack outfit belonged to ex-Spice Girl Geri Halliwell. Made by her sister Karen for Ginger Spice to wear at the 1997 Brits musical awards, Halliwell finally auctioned her minute mini at Sotheby's for a children's charity. It reached an astounding $69,000 – the biggest amount raised that night. Later that year, a young Spice Girls fan in

Flying the flag was never the same after Ginger Spice Girl Geri Halliwell's mini dress, 1997.

Mods in Brighton show that flag fashion was alive and kicking, 1982.

Avoid AT ALL COSTS **Anything**

. . . corduroy – poor man's velvet

Northern Ireland's County Down had her birthday party spoilt when she was asked to change out of her imitation of Geri's Union Jack dress for fear that it might provoke a Catholic/Protestant riot. The Union Jack is best kept on the flagpole where it belongs.

No Hiding Place

Camouflage

US Big Brother contestant and 'grunge' fan Jennifer Dedmon, clearly not on her way to join up, 2004.

After a flurry of fashionability for fancy uniform jackets in the mid-1960s, the whole military movement went out to battle. Army surplus stores such as the famous Laurence Corner in North London's Hampstead Road found themselves fighting off teenage youths desperate for the latest wartime gear. But it was not until the 1980s that camouflage, or Disruptive-Patterned Material (DPM) as it should correctly be known, became the *dernier cri* among top designers. Did they know that every army has a different pattern of DPM? Or that in the first Gulf War the British had to re-design their desert

Avoid AT ALL COSTS **Anything**

. . . lacy – only for underwear

camouflage into a new two-colour style after they found out the Iraqis had bought a job lot of their old four-colour design?

Camouflage on the high street does the opposite of what it is supposed to do. It draws attention to the wearer and definitely does not disguise them. When we know you have not joined up, what is the point of wearing grungy colours in violent abstract shapes? Designers should remember that camouflage was first intended for hiding tanks and troop supplies. Then it became the badge of every serving soldier down to the cook and the pen-pushers. Looking like the bark on a peeling plane tree was not, and never should be, high fashion.

Tell it to the Marines: this was never regulation gear, 1971.

Kings and queens of worst fashion

1. Abba
2. Elton John
3. Peter Wyngarde
4. Sarah, Duchess of York
5. Rod Stewart
6. Slade
7. The Bay City Rollers
8. Elizabeth Taylor
9. Mick Jagger
10. Paul Gascoigne

Worst fashion looks of the decades

1950s	Men's greaser look
	Women's beehive look
1960s	Men's 'drainpipe' look
	Women's hippie look
1970s	Men's 'big everything' look
	Women's 'flower power' look
1980s	Men's white suit look
	Women's 'power shoulder' look
1990s	Men's checked trousers look
	Women's camouflage look

Worst men's fashions

1. Handbags
2. Kipper ties
3. Dungarees
4. Tank tops
5. Bellbottoms
6. Flares
7. Fake fur coats
8. Safari suits
9. Bermuda shorts
10. Men's jumpers

BIG
isn't always best

One of the most unlikely endorsements was when Luciano Pavarotti launched a plethora of fragrances back in the 1990s, all of which failed. His voice may have been sensational, but his size didn't reach the high note with the sense of smell of Luciano Pavarotti (1994), Pavarotti Donna (1995) or Luciano (1999). Perhaps it was the barrel-shaped bottles that put the punters off.

Worst women's fashions

1. Dungarees
2. Power shoulders
3. Leggings
4. Legwarmers
5. Shell suits
6. Catsuits
7. Ski pants
8. Hot pants
9. Boob tubes
10. Knitted dresses

Worst fashion advertising partnerships

Arnold Palmer – Du Pont's Orlon synthetic fibre	1960s
Una Stubbs – ICI's Terylene fabric	1960s
Roger Daltry of The Who – Kickers shoes	1970s
Lord Sebastian Coe – C&A chain stores	1970s
Lulu – Freemans mail order catalogue	1970s
Jimmy Savile – Chukka shoes	1970s
Lorraine Chase – Grattan's mail order catalogue	1980s
O.J. Simpson – Dingo boots	1980s
Frankie Dettori – Jockey underpants	1990s
Pierce Brosnan – Maidenform bras	1990s

Worst fashion accessories

Ankle bracelets – didn't they once mean something different?

Banana clips – they didn't stay in – so out they went

Charm bracelets – they took so long to collect

Feather boas – fly away, fly away

Friendship bracelets – where did I put my half?

ID bracelets – move over, Mr T

Mood rings – a collector's item, surely?

Motif tops – definitely naff-naff

Facial piercing – hope the hole closed up

Swatch watches – how many watches can you have?

Where to Find out More

The following are some of the many sources I have found useful in compiling this book.

Cawthorne, Nigel *et al. Key Moments in Fashion. The Evolution of Style*, Hamlyn, 1998

Cox, Caroline. *Good Hair Days. A History of British Hairstyling*, Quartet, 1999

De la Haye, Amy, and Dingwell, Cathie. *Surfers Soulies Skinheads & Skaters. Subcultural Style from the Forties to the Nineties*, V & A, 1997

Fogg, Marnie. *Boutique. A '60s Cultural Phenomenon*, Mitchell Beazley, 2003

Goldberg, Michael Jay. *The Ties That Bind. Neckties 1945–1975*, Schiffer, Atglen, PA, 1997

Gorman, Paul. *The Look. Adventures in Pop and Rock Fashion*, Sanctuary, 2002

Larson, Mark. *The Mullet. Hairstyle of the Gods*, Barney Hoskyns, 1999

Polhemus, Ted. *Style Surfing. What to Wear in the 3rd Millennium*, Thames & Hudson, 1996

—. *Street Style from Sidewalk to Catwalk*, Thames & Hudson, 1997

Roach, Martin. *Dr. Martens. The Story of an Icon*, Chrysalis, 2003

Sims, Joshua. *Rock Fashion*, Omnibus Press, 1999

Wilson, Elizabeth and Taylor, Lou. *Through the Looking Glass. A History of Dress from 1860 to the Present Day*, BBC, 1989

For true vintage horror bloodhounds, the internet is chock-full of information, memories and opinions. Although no longer being added to, http://www.yesterdayland.com is still a goldmine. Http://www.fashion-era.com is an all-purpose dress history site that has good information on changing trends. Http://www.badfads.com is full of just what it says. To check out what happened in the various decades, visit http://www.bbc.co.uk/cults/ilove and http://www.nostalgiacentral.com. Other decade sites include http://www.sixtiescity.com/fashion, http://www.inthe70s.com; http://www.intheeighties.com, http://www.eightyeightynine.com for the 1980s, and http://www.inthe90s.com. Online vintage clothes selling site http://www.vintageblues.com has a good History of Fashion link at the bottom of its home page, as does http://www.fashion-flashbacks.com. Individual items often have websites set up by amateur devotees such as the addresses given for mullet hairstyles and toe socks. The search engine http://www.google.com is always the best place to start.

Finally, visit this book's website, http://www.worstfashions.com, and make your own contribution to this catalogue of horrors over the last fifty years. Your photographs and memories will help to build this site into the definitive research site for anyone interested in What We Shouldn't Have Worn ... But Did.

Enough to make you saddle-sore: suede horrors from the 1970s.

Acknowledgements and Picture Credits

Thanks go to everyone who helped me with the research for this project, in particular:
Joanna Norman, Pandora Ltd; Katherine Baird, London College of Fashion, University of the
Arts London; Beverley Cook, Museum of London; Diane Almond, The Woolmark Company;
staff at The Advertising Archives, Getty Images, Rex Features, and Brylcreem – Sara Lee,
H & BC UK; Natasha Thompson, BBC Worldwide; Katy Barwise, Hannah Greig, Adrianne
Leman, Liz Linning, David Shariatmadari and my daughters, Dominique, Katy and Emily.

I would like to credit the following illustration sources:
The Advertising Archives: pp. 11(r), 13(l), 16, 17(l), 17(r), 18, 20, 21(l), 23(l), 23(r), 24, 25(r),
29(l), 29(r), 33(r), 36, 37, 39(r), 40, 41, 43, 46, 47, 50, 51, 53(l), 54, 55, 58, 59, 61(r), 63, 71, 73,
75(r), 77, 81(l), 82, 83(l), 91, 97(r), 98, 99(r), 100, 101(l), 103(l), 104, 105, 110, 121, 122, 125,
129, 130, 134, 135, 136, 139(r), 156, 157(r), 161(r), 165(l).

Author's collection: pp. 1, 2, 6, 7, 9, 10, 11(l), 12(r), 19, 34, 44, 45, 48, 54(r), 56, 57, 61(l), 64, 72,
79, 84, 85(l), 86, 87(r), 102, 115(r), 119, 137, 152, 154, 155(r), 158, 159(l), 160, 162, 163(l),
163(r), 177, 179.

Getty Images: pp. 12, 14, 15(r), 22, 26, 28, 30, 31, 32, 35(r), 38, 39(l), 42, 49, 52, 60, 62, 65(l),
65(r), 74, 75(l), 76, 78, 81, 83(r), 85(r), 88, 89(t), 89(b), 90, 92, 93(l), 95, 96, 99(r), 101(r), 106,

107, 108, 109, 111, 112, 113(l), 113(r), 114, 115(l), 116, 117, 118, 120, 123, 128, 131(l), 131(r), 132, 133(l), 133(r), 139(l), 140, 142, 143, 144, 145, 146, 148, 150, 151(t), 151(b), 153(l), 153(r), 155(l), 157(l), 159(r), 161(l), 164, 165(r), 166, 168, 169.

Rex Features: pp. 15(l), 21(r), 25(l), 27, 35(l), 66, 67, 68, 69, 70, 80, 87(l), 93(r), 94, 97(l), 103(r), 124, 126, 127, 138, 141, 147, 149(l), 149(r), 167(l), 167(r).

The Woolmark Company: p. 33(l).

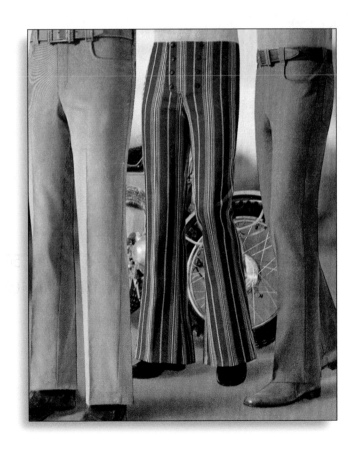

How did they stay up? Synthetic strides, *c.* 1970.

Index

Page numbers in italic refer to individual personalities.